HOW TO DATE MEN

WHEN YOU HATE MEN

HOW | WHEN
TO | YOU
DATE | HATE
MEN | MEN

Blythe Roberson

FLATIRON
BOOKS
NEW YORK

www.flatironbooks.com

Designed by Susan Walsh

The Library of Congress Cataloging-in-Publication Data is available upon request.

ISBN 978-1-250-19342-1 (hardcover)
ISBN 978-1-250-19344-5 (ebook)

Our books may be purchased in bulk for promotional, educational, or business
use. Please contact your local bookseller or the Macmillan Corporate and
Premium Sales Department at 1-800-221-7945, extension 5442, or by email at
MacmillanSpecialMarkets@macmillan.com.

First Edition: January 2019

10   9   8   7   6   5   4   3   2   1

For my family, who should not read this book

Contents

HOW TO DATE MEN

WHEN YOU HATE MEN

INTRODUCTION

INTRODUCTION

think about men all the time. About how they, individually (Donald Trump) and as a group, are oppressing me. And about how they, individually (Timothée Chalamet) and as a group, are very hot. And also: how spending so much time thinking about how they, as a group, are hot . . . is probably oppressing me. Unsure what else to do about it, I've written this book.

How to Date Men When You Hate Men is a comedy philosophy book about what dating and loving are like now, in an era that we thought was the end of patriarchy (but we now know is at least five hundred years away from that) and at the beginning of an age where robots do all our dating for us. Honestly: it often sucks, and it's hard to know if it's because of my personality, the guy's personality, or thousands of years of inequality stemming from gender imbalances created by plow farming. This book is loosely structured to mirror the arc of a relationship, from crushes to flirting, dating and encountering problems, getting serious, breaking up, being single, and . . . making art about it all! Ah, yes: the human life span.

"DO YOU REALLY HATE ALL MEN???" ask you, Bill Maher. I don't! Some of my closest friends are men! I have, and love, many male family members: all of my siblings are boys, and there are seemingly thousands of them (there are five). And of course, there are men who I have kissed and cared about or who I am dying to kiss and care about. Almost universally, I still feel fondly toward any guy I've ever been romantically interested in or involved with. These men are funny and interesting. Some are really kind! Many are hot! Quite a few still to this day very generously fave my social media content. To paraphrase the suffragettes in *Mary Poppins*: though I adore men as individuals, I believe that as a group they're systemically oppressing women.

We're at a point where it's clear that patriarchy exists and that gender roles—the concept of gender, even—is profoundly broken. I won't sit here and PROVE patriarchy to you, like my high school crush once asked me to (specifically telling me to cite more statistics and be less emotional—but more on that later!). Honestly, it's not the responsibility of the oppressed person to constantly explain the details of their oppression to their oppressor, and it's not like oppressors don't have the same Google everyone else does. Also, I think that if you picked up a book with a title about hating men, you're already pretty hip to the ubiquity of sexism and toxic masculinity. Young men are taking guns to school and shooting their classmates. An extremely high percentage of any men you've ever heard of have recently been revealed to lie somewhere on the spectrum of creepy to sexual criminal. Our president is constantly talking about the size of his penis! I feel certain it is only a matter of time before he has the surgeon general release a glowing report on it! Men: they need to get their shit together!

Let me take a moment to specify who exactly I am talking about when I say "men." I am talking in most cases about straight, cis, able-bodied white men. I'm talking about men who have all the privilege in the world and who don't even realize it because this is their water, to quote a classic example of a straight, cis, white man (who I love! If you'd asked me who my favorite author was at any point between 2011 and 2015, I would have said David Foster Wallace and then tried to figure out if you had read *Infinite Jest* without straight-up asking if you had read *Infinite Jest*). There are so many different systems of privilege—race, gender identity, sexuality, class, education, body shape, and on and on—that all interact to affect how much power a person has and how oppressed other people are by that power. The practice of considering these various identities in context with one another is called intersectionality, a term coined by Kimberlé Crenshaw in 1989. If I wrote out "straight, cis, able-bodied, upper-class, college-educated, conventionally attractive white men" every time I meant "straight, cis, able-bodied, upper-class, college-educated, conventionally attractive white men," my book would be 1,100 pages long. It's not, because unlike straight, cis, able-bodied, upper-class, college-educated, conventionally attractive white men, I know how to edit a book.

But I should also say this: I'm a white, straight, cis, able-bodied, college-educated woman. I, too, have a lot of privilege! This doesn't mean that I'm immune to stuff like male privilege and gender discrimination and hot boys manipulating me over text with an almost psychology-experiment level of efficacy. It means that there are types of dating-adjacent discrimination I have never experienced, and that what I have experienced has probably not been as bad as it would have been if my privilege were less. In this book, I write about how women are reduced to their worth as sexual bodies—this has always been worse for black women and women of color. I write about not knowing if I want to get married—but I've never had to live in a country that told me I *couldn't* marry because of my sexual orientation. Even just having the free time to go out with dudes and spend money on food and drinks and tickets to see Antoni from *Queer Eye* host a comedy show—it's a privilege. This is all to say that straight white men are not the only ones who need to do work! Fifty-three percent of white women voted for Trump; we really need to have a group meeting and reevaluate our commitment to not being villains to everyone. As people who do face discrimination but also have a lot of privilege, we have a responsibility to use our privilege to . . . dismantle our privilege.

This book is about my personal experiences as a horned-up perv but also about the "patriarchy" part of "white-supremacist capitalist patriarchy," a phrase I say so often in conversation that I hope at least one of my friends has made it my personal text tone. It's a book about the experience of loving while living through this oil-slick puddle of an era, specifically being a woman attracted to men who have all this structural power over you and have been told for millennia that it's cool to treat women in a very degrading way, consciously or subconsciously. It's not that there are "good men" versus "bad men" (though there are some obvious monsters): all men have received this coding. They aren't born evil, they're born into an evil system! It just didn't sound as catchy to name the book *How to Date Men When They Are Born into and Brainwashed by an Evil System That Mightily Oppresses Women.*

But the pitfalls of dating in the patriarchy go beyond the obvious, like sexual assault. How do you date men when they don't want to date anyone more successful than they are? How do you express excitement about love when men call that being "boy crazy"? Why get married when marriage benefits men in almost every way but makes women more likely to die a violent death? That's absolutely true, and knowing that, I find it makes so little sense to get married, and yet I still bought a fake engagement ring at CVS for nine dollars this weekend. There's a lot to sort through!

Meanwhile, men are finally learning that it's actually not cool to act like giant, predatory chodes to every female-presenting human they encounter. Listen, I don't feel sympathy for men who ruin women's lives because they decide they have a right to the body, time, or labor of any woman they want. But I can understand why the average man might feel unsteady and confused, seeing as all media and authority figures have told them their whole lives that it was fine for them to behave in a certain way, a way that doesn't really take female agency or interiority or personhood into consideration. Men read a lot of J. D. Salinger and grew up on *Annie Hall*, I get it! Please, men, have a seat in my cacti-and-throw-pillow-strewn salon and take a read on how it feels to love from the other side of things. Use it as a template for how to love women and how to flirt and be sexual in a way that won't ruin women's lives, or—and this is such a recent possibility—your life! Learn how the algorithm we've been coded into works, and help us change it.

The current, very overdue acknowledgment of widespread sexual harassment, paired with an increase in the number of women who are able to support themselves, paired with a million other things, means we're experiencing large-scale social change in how we date, how we structure our lives, how genders interact, and in what "gender" even means, if it in fact exists at all!! It's easy to feel confused about how dating is supposed to go and/or worthless because you feel like you're not living up to the standard. But I've begun to believe we're just blindly ripping our way through giant jungle cobwebs on our way to a new world order, and the fact that I am twenty-seven and not married or significantly partnered says more about our times than it does about me. I also feel like a fraud in using a lot of terms that used to be tied to more easily defined experiences, like "date" or "breakup." I know that most of the time I'm not using those terms in a way that would make sense to previous generations. But the fact remains that I am having experiences, and I need to describe them! And maybe they don't *really* get what I'm actually talking about when I say "date," but it's a lot closer than if I just started making up my own terms and telling people that some cute guy and I went on a blorg.

My hope for dating is higher than being able to kiss a man without both of us spontaneously combusting due to the problematicness of it all. I aim to experience romance joyfully—free not just from the issues that stem from patriarchy but from the anxiety of being a person at all. Is that possible? And what would that joyful relationship look like?

In addition to being a woman who loves men specifically, I'm also just a human person who loves human people. Not every single one of my thoughts/tweets/breaths/farts is, like, Mediated Through My Gender Identity. This book is not just about straight female romantic love; it's also about romantic love in general. In fact, it was originally inspired by a book I love (and that you should, too: Lorde tweeted about it): *A Lover's Discourse* by Roland Barthes, a male human person who loved other male human people. I bought the book in the summer of 2015, in an Amazon order that also included a giant bottle of children's mouthwash, because fellas: I was ready to kiss. I spent most of my time that summer with a guy who I was totally in love with, though it would be about four months before I ruined everything by *realizing* that I was in love with that guy. In *A Lover's Discourse* Barthes takes various words associated with being a lover—"engulfment," "waiting," "why?"—and writes in fragments about his own thoughts and about literature, philosophy, whatever else that relates. I felt extremely indicted by some sections: "Even as he obsessively asks himself why he is not loved, the amorous subject lives in the belief that the loved object does love him but does not tell him so." Save yourself the trouble of reading any of my previous work; that quote sums it up! But I also finished the book wanting more. Barthes didn't cover the specifics of a lot of stuff that I'm interested in, like trying to kiss a gender that is actively oppressing you, or, like: texting is hard. Additionally, it DID very extensively cover

The Sorrows of Young Werther, which I do not care about and never will!

So here's the book I wished I had read, about not just dating but love in general: *A Lover's Discourse* but considering patriarchy and technology and how changing gender roles and economies and urbanization have morphed how two humans decide to love each other and structure that love, and also with jokes. Like *A Lover's Discourse,* the bulk of this book consists of words and phrases— "being chill," "professionally insecure woke boys," "subtweets"— with a few pages of thoughts and definitions on each, from my own life and from TV and literature and from possible futures I have imagined with Timothée Chalamet. Interspersed are comedy pieces that build to no particular point but that I included for fun and because the world needs to know that Tom Hanks is the villain of *You've Got Mail.*

Is this book a "how to" book? No. Honestly, I am bad at dating and all men hate me as much as I hate them (they hate me for reasons that are less structural), so I have no advice to give. Like, truly: I didn't date at all in high school or college. I've never had an official boyfriend, which used to make me very concerned that something was seriously wrong with me, but now I'm like, sure, whatever, it's likely that something is seriously wrong with me, but I'm too iron-deficient to care. Also, I love myself anyways, and maybe this is just some generational shift, like how millennials don't buy houses because we're too busy buying avocado toast and also because the economy is wrecked. I do see dudes casually and sometimes for a long period of time, but I'm bad at that, too. I've gotten dumped on a crowded subway, *recently.* I regularly give

NO indication of my attraction to men until it becomes very obvious that they're not into me, at which time I make a grand declaration of Feelings in such a way that it becomes a Big Deal.

Plus, dating advice is boring and I don't care about it. And advice books seem to be weirdly gendered—women are made to give solutions to discrete, manageable situations, whereas men get to write philosophical grand thoughts that are no immediate help to anyone. Like, Plato's *Symposium* contains a story about soul mates: human beings were originally four-legged, four-armed, two-faced beings who had immense strength and were always cartwheeling around, perfectly content. To prevent these powerful humans from taking over, the gods split each human into two, who then wandered the earth looking for their soul mates. That is . . . the dumbest thing I've ever heard.

I want to claim the male privilege of being no help at all. Honestly, by default, I will probably be more helpful than Plato. Here's a book made up of so many opinions all clumped together that they just might have congealed into some sort of worldview. So consider this a philosophy book, and please add me to your college syllabi.

I wrote this book hoping that I would work through all my feelings and get all my thoughts in a straight line and never have to write or think about dating again. I wanted to write this one book about love and then be done with it, so when future people ask me how I feel about men or dating I could just say, "Read the book!" I did worry that choosing to write about love was in a way participating in my own oppression, writing about a frivolous topic instead of something meaningful, like . . . nuclear proliferation? I was like: Can't women write about anything other than dating and their anxiety disorders? And then I was like [writes book about dating].

But I also think women are raised to think about love all the time! I grew up watching Nora Ephron's better rom-coms and reading Jane Austen's better marriage-plot novels, stories where the plot is driven by love, everyone is funny, and the men always kind of suck, even when they're played by Colin Firth in the movie version. (Although I didn't realize the men kind of sucked for, like, a solid ten years; realizing the men suck is a significant milestone in a modern feminist awakening.) Also conditioning me to think constantly about love: Women's magazines. TV and films (I watch a lot: my literal day job is as a celebrity researcher on a late-night talk show). Every person I know constantly asking me if there are any special men in my life. (ALL men are special, you liberal cucks!)

So honestly, I've thought about love a lot because YOU MADE ME THIS WAY. And my thoughts on it: are good. I've come to see talking about love as similar to sharing everyone's salaries, or to holding consciousness-raising sessions. We need to talk about our experiences so that we know what's normal and so that we can identify patterns of oppression and figure out ways to overturn them. And also, I never understand ANY text ANY man sends me and I NEED the collective brainpower of Earth's women to figure out how to respond.

1

CRUSHES

Joy

It seems to me that the meaning of life is to treat everyone with kindness and to be as joyful as possible. I mean, it's either that or to buy a ton of yachts.

Certainly the only worthwhile or even bearable way to experience love and romance and [spits on the ground for fifteen minutes] DATING is joyfully. But due to the insane amount of cultural narratives and patriarchal power imbalance and beauty-myth bullshit that surround love, it can be VERY DIFFICULT to operate in this way. It's like trying to kiss your sweet crush while a cement mixer operated by Woody Allen is dumping raccoons on you. If you can manage to exist in the moment, this beautiful thing is happening (kissing), but it's insane to expect anyone could focus on that while society is telling us all these crazy stories about how love happens and giving one partner tons of structural power over the other, all while telling the partner with less power that they NEED to secure the affections of the one with more power.

(In my analogy, this is all translates to raccoons methodically tangling your hair with the intelligence they use to open Pringles cans and unzip tents.) And in addition to all that, Woody Allen exists. (Your sweet crush is definitely NOT IN SUPPORT of Woody Allen, but he can't help mentioning how formative *Annie Hall* was for him.)

But what is life but fifteen to one hundred years of becoming cocooned in societal bullshit, followed by zero to eighty-five years of sloughing off that bullshit through reading, therapy, and sitting on the edge of a lake thinking about your life and choices? And when we've sat at that lake long enough and fully sloughed, we will be as we were when we were pure children, when we had never heard about thigh gaps and we could talk to animals and breathe underwater. So how exactly does that sloughing happen, that ridding ourselves of all the crusty scum that's covering up our ability to find joy?

For a while I thought this joy could be achieved by getting rid of all of my negativity about love. Maybe I'd use transcendental meditation techniques to recognize and dismiss any thoughts about whether it would make sense to put my Emmys next to my husband's Pulitzer before I had even kissed this aspiring novelist yet. (Also, I would be the one winning a Pulitzer—for playwriting—as well as two Nobels, for literature and peace.) Admittedly, I have never studied transcendental meditation, but I've researched enough celebrities who have vaguely described it in interviews that I feel like I get the general idea. I'd use this same technique when I started worrying if I'm too ugly to deserve love or when I acted obsessively. Or maybe I would stop all this not through meditation but just by being too beaten down by current events to think about anything else. I discovered that I don't have *time* to feel bad about myself when I'm so busy frantically texting friends about John Bolton and GETTING NO RESPONSES.

But just getting rid of negative thoughts isn't the same as being joyful. Being devoid of negativity is more like successfully "being chill," a relationship stage that inspires not spontaneous dancing and smiles but a lot of lying completely still on the couch next to but not looking at your phone. Certainly it is important to slough off all that fucked-up societal shit—it definitely stands in the way of joy—but creating a bullshit deficit does not necessarily mean that joy will rush in. There aren't many models of joyful, nonneurotic romance in pop culture that I can think of, I guess because it wouldn't be interesting enough to sustain a whole book or TV show or movie (maybe there's some indie British movie, but I don't have a streaming service powerful enough to find it). Without stories and examples to draw on, that mind-set isn't going to just magically percolate into our brains. So how *do* we go about finding the fantastic and lovely and fun side of romance that, theoretically, got us so obsessed with it in the first place?

Candidly—I don't know. I think probably it's down to some very Zen shit like living in each discrete moment as if your heart and brain spread out across the entire Earth and simultaneously were the smallest, densest atom in existence and every quark in that atom were LOVING this exact cup of coffee. Again, from what I've learned from reading all those celebrity interviews, this is probably mindfulness. I know that advice is so trite that it's maddening, like when the *Women's Health* magazine that showed up to my house every month even though I hadn't subscribed said that menstrual cramps could be solved by exercise. I GUESS that's scientifically true and obvious, but have you considered: I'd rather take an enormous knife and cut out my uterus than put on workout pants? But it seems that, unfortunately, the best way to find joy in romance is to always be alert to, to experience, and to expect joy in every aspect of your life. If you don't have a happy, healthy relationship template to follow, you have to stay present in the moment and essentially make it up for yourself as you go along. Extremely difficult, I know! The whole point of narratives is so we don't have to invent human behavior anew every generation. But remember: the Neanderthals did it, and they were a lot dumber than you!

The other reason that dating feels obligatory to me is that I want to make art about romance. I was raised by a mom who owned, like, four total VHS tapes, three of which were *When Harry Met Sally . . .* , *Sense and Sensibility*, and *You've Got Mail*. (The fourth was . . . *Fly Away Home*?) It is not exaggerating to say I have seen those movies a combined total of one hundred times, less than 10 percent of which was making guys watch them with me, as a flirt. Those movies are a part of who I am. They are the kind of art I like and the kind of art I want to make: art about people falling in love, and more specifically, art about Meg Ryan falling in love with men who don't deserve her.

But it's essential to not view romance as this obligatory, chore-like thing you have to "solve" to advance to the next level. Which is hard! There is definitely less societal pressure to get married now, since I no longer need a man to get a credit card and spend all my money on shoes that I saw Harry Styles wear. But there's still a lot of pressure to be partnered—not just to be married but even just to have some sort of partner to gossip to your coworkers about or take as a plus one to all manner of friends', family's, and rich acquaintances' weddings. I personally feel like a socially inept goblin for never having had a boyfriend. I feel like it screams out SHE IS BROKEN AND BAD. Which I know is not true. I *am* a goblin, sure, but only because I am small, mischievous, and greedy for gold and jewelry. But that pressure can build up until it becomes a frantic need to acquire a partner, *any partner,* and while some people would say that look is unattractive, I say: Who cares whether it's attractive. It's just not fun!

To feel joyful about love, you have to feel that you've opted into it, not that you've been forced to participate in it through your decision to be born. Alexandra Molotkow has written of Carly Rae Jepsen: "Jepsen is old enough to be cynical, but she isn't; she's not some cloying naif, either, but a person who has opted into romance because it is a joy." Opting into romance! Because it is a joy! I don't want to opt out, so instead I'm trying to opt in with as much weird intensity as I want and to not feel bad about it.

Crushes

I have many crushes, a collection which I love and nurture. I like to think of all my crushes as a bunch of gemstones I've acquired primarily because they're pretty and then also because they have rumored magical properties. They give me joy in their sheer multitude and they look great when featured on my Instagram.

Patriarchy places way too much (and mostly negative) import on women's crushes. They're frivolous, distracting women from serious matters like, I guess, soil composition? There's a perception that a woman who has a lot of crushes must be some kind of demented perv (as if this were a bad thing). And due to economy of characters or ease of tracking a woman's desires or just the incorrect assumption that women are naturally monogamous, society assumes that if a woman has a crush, OH BOY she is COMING FOR THAT CRUSH and for EVOLUTIONARY REASONS she is trying to get that man's sperm and trick him into raising a child with her for THE REST OF HIS NATURAL LIFE.

Which is all just so wrong. My two main Feelings regarding crushes are (1) fun and (2) who cares. The only accurate representation of this that I have ever seen in any, ANY studio film is in *Ghostbusters*, when Kristen Wiig correctly perceives that Chris Hemsworth is Very Good Looking. It's silly and a running joke and about the fortieth-most-important thing about her character. Her crush doesn't mean that she's desperate and it doesn't undermine her in any way. And, I think, after five thousand–plus years of men writing about their muses, women are owed a couple hundred years at least to talk openly about Oscar Isaac's thicc legs.

I mean, yes, there are unhealthy ways to crush. There are ways for your crush to fill you with net bad energy, like you're coming down with a fever, and not the net good Pure Crush energy that feels like singing "Teenage Dirtbag" at karaoke and announcing to everyone that you have only ever heard the One Direction version of this song. I had this kind of net bad crush in high school.

I was a teen and everything was already heightened, which people think is because of hormones but for me was also because of my maniacal addiction to Fun Dip. It was the only candy I cared about, and I never experienced a sugar crash because my fourteen-year-old body was too powerful and also probably because I never went long enough without eating Fun Dip for my blood sugar levels to drop. In the way that surfers and Nancy Meyers characters who live on the beach are always finding sand in their shoes, I would find Fun Dip in the pockets of all my clothes. Put on an old jacket I hadn't worn since the previous winter, absolutely no chance I'd find five dollars, but almost 100 percent chance there would be Fun Dip in there. I was hyper for the entirety of the 2000s.

On top of all of that ready-made energy, I was under the impression that it was proper to have only one crush at a time. So after much consideration I got serious and chose to love just one boy who would never love me. For the next four years, for this boy, I pretended I cared about the Manning family of football fame. I read the books he said were his favorite books. I posted Facebook statuses of the most absolutely dramatic as possible Taking Back Sunday lyrics, *with no attribution*. This boy and I giggled through AP Bio and got separated and seated on opposite sides of the class for talking too much, and then we got in more trouble for creepily staring and smiling at one another from across the room. I spent a lot of time justifying to my friends why he wasn't really a jerk and why he had to keep dating his conventionally hot, popular, Christian girlfriend. I did this for the entirety of high school, and it did not nourish me in any way. It didn't even lead to any good art, because back then I thought I was going to grow up to be president. (This was before we knew that women are not allowed to be president.)

AND THEN, a couple years after college, I drove down three hours from a vacation in Seattle to get a drink with this high school crush in Portland. We started talking about feminism, and it turned out he had never heard of "privilege," and when I explained it he was just NOT having any of it: he, a white man, hadn't gotten everything he'd wanted in life, and he'd lived through some personal tragedy, so how could he have any structural advantages that women and people of color and poor people didn't? And I was like, "UHHHH BUT" and "WELL HELLO" and "RACISM IS A SYSTEM" and ultimately he told me, and I am quoting: "You've changed a lot since high school. You've gotten angry. I don't like the person you've become."

Coming from the person who I had spent 45 percent of the years 2004–2009 thinking about, this was so devastating that it was almost hilarious. I did not know that people told other people they didn't like the person they'd become, outside of superhero movies when the superhero comes too close to using their power for evil. I rushed out of Portland, pulling over as soon as I got out of the city to pee and to text everyone who had ever met both me and my crush but who definitely liked me more.

All of which is to say, you know . . . maybe it's healthier to have a lot of crushes who diffuse your crush energy than just one. That laser focus can be caustic, causing you to overly invest in that person and in the narratives about them you've created. But spread out over fifty men yelling "I am crush!" like at the end of *Spartacus*, it's a fun, flirty, and fine amount of energy and everyone walks away happy. That's how *Spartacus* ends, right?

I LOVE to think about my many millions of crushes. I love to think of them as a small work group assembled to do my bidding. I love to think about whole countries populated by my crushes: somewhere remote, like the Faroe Islands, my crushes in cable-knit sweaters drinking coffee from ceramic mugs, all on their best behavior and somehow never figuring out that they all know me.

I love when too many of my crushes show up at a party! Oh no! My many crushes! Interacting! It's like later seasons of *Game of Thrones* when your fan favorites meet up for the first time, but I'm the only fan and I might really kiss all of them, and right now I need all but one of them to go home.

I once had a party with too many crushes and one of my crushes called an Uber Pool to leave and when it pulled up, a man leaned out the window and yelled "Blythe??! Roberson?" Another one of my crushes.

I highly recommend having enough crushes for them to meet in the wild and go off on their own adventures.

"But I don't know millions of crushes," says you, with your eyes closed, walking repeatedly into a wall. Listen: taking the most openhearted and generous view of the universe, everyone is attractive and we're all just dogs doing our best. Everybody has a whole universe inside of them if you can get them talking about the things they like (everyone except . . . Jason Segel). If you pay attention, a lot of people are interesting in a "perhaps we should be licking each other's tongues???" sort of way.

It's Not About You

The lovely thing about crushes is that they're not really about the person who is being crushed on at all! Sorry, my crushes: as is true of everything, this is all about Blythe Roberson! (Me, not the teen named Blythe Roberson who follows me on Instagram and is much hotter and much richer than I am.)

Crushes are basically love energy within yourself that you use the idea of another person to access. They're potential love energy, as opposed to the kinetic love energy of a relationship that's actually happening. The platonic ideal of this completely-about-the-crusher crush are crushes you have as a child—what are you going to do with a fifth grader, even if he has a crush on you back?—or crushes on celebrities, who you know you will never meet, and in fact do not want to meet because it would shatter the illusion and ruin everything. (Once I was walking on the sidewalk just as Tom Hiddleston came out a door three feet away from me, and in order to avoid meeting him I instinctively turned and walked straight into traffic.) But potential energy crushes are just as valid when they're an adult woman having a crush on a man in her actual life. This potential energy is accessed through imagining and projecting.

Imagining: Let's say I'm about to fall asleep, or I'm on a train and I'm tired of reading my depressing book about the apocalypse, or I'm seeing a play where it's all out-of-context quotes from *Star Trek*, which sounded great in theory but in actuality makes me regret being born. I use those (and many other!) moments to think about my current crush and imagine every stage of our relation-ship, from first kiss to informing our friends that we're dating to me winning an Emmy to him deciding he wants to retire super early (oh no!) to us convincing five quality friends to move to Montana with us to all seven of us falling into a gorge together and dying.

"WHY??! WOULD YOU . . . IMAGINE THESE DETAILED THINGS about someone you BARELY KNOW . . . YOU . . . CREEP?"—you. Well, I think part of it is that sports psychology thing where you visualize yourself doing your tennis serve two hundred times, and then when you do it you REALLY DO perform better. That's a true thing! And I'd add to that: I imagine the full course of relationships with hot men because it is #fun as hell to imagine a love with someone before I get to know that someone and he fucks it all up with his actual-person-existing-everyday-ness. In my mind he is very polite and doesn't have even a tiny amount of subconscious learned hatred of women. He texts back promptly, and our relationship progresses in a steady and linear way. It's very entertaining!

Projecting is less about entertainment/a way to kill forty-five dreadful minutes at the theater and more about using the idea of another person to figure out what you find important in a lover. Tavi Gevinson has written beautifully (see: all of the website Rookie dot com) about how fandom is ultimately about the fan. She uses the example of boy bands, which intentionally try to be blank slates that girls can project their desires onto. That's why all the boys seem vaguely nice and all the lyrics are extremely forget-table. (How insanely banal are the lyrics? My friend Fran Hoepf-ner and I knew for years that we wanted to get matching One

Direction tattoos, but we couldn't figure out what to get because all the lyrics are bad and all the song titles are bad.) The boys present as archetypes (Niall is the bro-y one, Harry is the artsy one, Louis is the one who had a baby with a "very close friend") that young girls can choose between, narrowing and recognizing their taste before they have to start choosing between actual boys in nonlaboratory environments. Boy bands essentially presenting themselves as canvases for young female minds *bothers* many men, who maybe DON'T GET what's happening and also have evolved an innate need to disparage things that are made specifically for women, especially if those women are young. They need to prove that they hate these women-targeted things, because society has taught men that young women are silly and stupid and worthless, so if men like things that young women like, those men are silly and stupid due to the transitive property. It's simple math, a thing which men love! This is all to say: the fact that he values young women is why Harry Styles should be president.

Using a crush to learn about yourself is even more obvious when you're a child, trying to carve an identity out of the marble slab of just "being a human who exists." Please, take a comfortable seat on your faux-leather recliner as I tell you about my first big, dumb, burning crush on a guy I'll call "Kyle," because that name is hilarious to me.

No experience in my life will ever match the sexual charge of middle school field trip bus rides: the sharp butterflies, the mania, the total presence and attention that I got whenever I was on a bus for an hour with Kyle.

Kyle was tall and skinny with a mass of curly brown hair. He was older: he was in the highest grade of our middle school (eighth) when I was in the lowest (sixth). He was vaguely artistic—first-chair trombone in the top band at school—but also pretty conventional. In other words: he was exactly my type. I didn't know this yet, because I didn't have a type yet. Kyle *created* my type. When I met him, I had no idea what hit me. I thought "obsessed with Kyle" would just be my personality for the rest of my life.

My mission in life became not to seduce Kyle exactly, because I was eleven and pretty much asexual. I couldn't even say the word "bra" out loud, and if Kyle had kissed me I probably would have cried from sensory overload. Instead my mission was to, like, absorb Kyle whole into my body. I was not operating from a place of power. I was so hyper that I would literally march around the halls with my best friend, Ariel, who was in marching band with Kyle and me. I was a know-it-all in constant search of trivia questions. One of my favorite outfits was a pink pastel shirt with pink pastel bell-bottoms, which I wore on heavy rotation until Kyle's cool eighth-grade friend Kait remarked, "Oh, you look adorable, but I'm too old to pull off that kind of look now."

Those middle school field trip bus rides gave me a controlled environment in which to really indulge in my giant, manic crush. I would sit as close as possible to Kyle without sitting next to him, because (a) who did I think I was and (b) I would probably have exploded if I sat next to him for an hour. Often I sat in the seat in front of him and constantly poked my head over the seat-back to make some comment, or sometimes I sat in the seat across from him and tried to look cool by sitting backward, or, in a horrible nightmare scenario, sometimes I sat two seats up and kitty corner, and desperately hung into the aisle trying to catch Kyle's attention while Ariel threw bits of my school supplies out the window to punish me for taking the better seat.

I was entirely alert and magnetized for every second of each of those field trip bus rides. I truly have never experienced anything like it. The closest analogue I can think of is the way rock stars describe the feeling they get from live performances—total connectivity and power, as if only onstage are they experiencing themselves fully. Their focus is so complete in the moment that they often cannot exactly remember their shows, and either because of something like this or because it has been sixteen years, I can't remember my bus rides with Kyle very substantially either. But I remember this: before one bus ride, I somehow came into possession of a small stuffed hippo. On the bus, Kyle pretended to be in love with the hippo. THE HIPPO BECAME A PRICELESS OBJECT TO ME AND I LITERALLY STILL HAVE THE HIPPO. IT IS IN MY DAD'S BASEMENT.

Here's what I don't remember: almost anything real about Kyle. I can conjure up almost nothing about his personality—which may be because no one has a personality in middle school, boys especially. I don't know much of what happened to Kyle after he graduated from our middle school. He must have gone to the same high school as me, but I have no memory of it. Kyle was a very large part of what I thought about from ages eleven to twelve. Now he is very hard to Google and it doesn't bother me.

What's important about Kyle is the insane way he made me feel. Being obsessed with Kyle was my introduction to dealing with romantic/obsessive feelings without actual reciprocity or even the possibility of reciprocity getting in the way. It helped me figure out *what* was so attractive about him, specifically, and what would be attractive to me generally for the next seven hundred years of my life. He was a very real, live, breathing boy, but he was also a whiteboard on which I figured a bunch of stuff out.

Very early-stage adult crushes are similar to those middle school crushes, or celebrity crushes. When all you know about a new (in-person) crush is that he's funny and he looks kind of like Jack Antonoff, that crush is also a blank slate onto which you can project anything. At this point, you're basically just a fan of an individual person you semi-know. You have an idea of them and you love it and it doesn't really matter how they feel about the situation, because you aren't bothering them—you're MAYBE talking to other women about it, but like you would talk about the new *Queer Eye* (TAN is the best one, never talk to me about Antoni!!!). Problems arise only when outside forces (read: the patriarchy) decide you're acting boy crazy.

Boy Crazy

Have you heard of *The Beauty Myth* by Naomi Wolf, perhaps from Tumblr or a women's studies class or from me personally knowing you for two seconds and screaming about how you should read it because it changed my life? It's a book about how our modern concept of beauty enforces a patriarchal system that oppresses women by telling them that they need to meet an impossible idea of beauty that is completely divorced from reality and based in white supremacy. You know, girl stuff!

Meeting or not meeting our culture's punitive beauty standards contributes to whether or not women get jobs, find love, are treated nicely by strangers. Women are harshly policed and punished if they don't conform—but if they do, they're called vain, shallow, selfish, insecure . . . dealer's choice of insults, really! The path women are expected to walk is narrow to the point of nonexistence, and the attempt requires constant thought and attention.

The quote that convinced me to read *The Beauty Myth*: "A culture fixated on female thinness is not an obsession about female beauty, but an obsession about female obedience. Dieting is the most potent political sedative in women's history; a quietly mad population is a tractable one." As someone who was hungry for two straight years in high school I can 100 percent confirm that I was at no point able to think about how to overthrow the patriarchy, or even to learn about patriarchy! I was almost exclusively thinking about cucumbers and ninety-calorie yogurts.

I bring up the Beauty Myth because *romance is the same thing, I think*.

I came to this conclusion when a guy was giving me strange signals for months and I was using my brain to its full capacity trying to figure out what the hell was going on. I realized: oh, this is a political issue, because instead of focusing on the intersectional-socialist-matriarchal revolution I've been focusing on whether or not what just happened was a date.

Society has told women *forever* that finding a partner is para-

mount. For much of history they HAD to find spouses, as an economic necessity! That's why Lizzie Bennet and Mr. Darcy's flirting
is so charged—if he doesn't decide he wants to marry her, she'll
eventually starve to death. As recently as the 1970s, women couldn't
even have their own credit cards—which, again, would lead to
me, at least, starving to death as I buy food only from Seamless.
Even today, there's constantly pressure to (a) find a partner and (b)
receive male validation, two separate but related things. That
pressure comes from countless facets of society: from friends and
family always asking about your love life, from a barrage of movies
and songs about pairing off, from constant coverage of whether
female celebrities have found a man yet or are brittle spinsters
bound to die alone. (Whereas men who date serially or not at all
are applauded for stepping out with their pussy posse.)

Women are surrounded by propaganda that stresses the importance of finding a partner in a way that forces us to think about it
constantly. We have an extra job at all times in a way that men
don't!

Maybe this fact accounts for some of the enduring popularity
of *The Bachelor*. The show re-creates this pressure in almost scientific conditions, depriving the women on the show of all external
stimuli (like internet access and phone calls) so that they have nothing to think about other than securing a man's affections. And the
entire premise of the show is that twenty-five TV-hot, fun young
women are competing for one boring, hot (in a boring way) Ben
Higgins (both the actual name of one of the bachelors and a com-
posite name of all the bachelors). "Oh, this is just like dating in New
York," I thought while watching the show: every "meh" guy here

has two thousand of the coolest women in the country trying to date him. But actually: that scarcity principle, created by alarmist articles like "THERE ARE SEVEN WOMEN IN NEW YORK FOR EVERY ONE DUDE," is meant to further panic women into focusing their attention on dating to the exclusion of, I don't know, unionizing? Given these tactics, it's not surprising that the women on *The Bachelor* scheme and cry. It's the logical response.

(Of course, many feminist women, myself included, enjoy watching *The Bachelor*. It's nice to watch a highly distilled version of the machinations used on you to make you crazy! And also, the locations are very beautiful, and the producers really do know how to egg everyone into acting extremely dramatic at all times. But I prefer *Unreal* to *The Bachelor*, since it reminds me that, oh yeah, I am being manipulated to be insane about love—a reminder I extremely appreciate!)

So when women do not have a partner they are punished and mocked. But if they do conform, and spend a lot of time thinking and talking about romance, they are called boy crazy. (Whereas men who care about romance aren't called girl crazy.) Like with the Beauty Myth, you're punished either way and again forced to attempt to walk an impossibly narrow path. The time and energy women have to spend negotiating all of this is why it is a political issue: it steals time we could have spent running for office, making money, or shorting the housing market in 2006 (I just watched *The Big Short* on a plane!). Hell, even if it just steals time I could have spent sitting in a hot tub trying to read and finding I can't because my hands are too wet: I'm still pissed. Men (aka a patriarchal society designed to benefit men) have tricked me into wasting a lot of time thinking about them, and I can never get that time back. But guess what, men: now I'm thinking about how to over-throw you.

One-Track Mind

The easiest way to turn a manageable, fun-size crush into an oversize, not-heavy-just-awkward, obsessive crush is to allow your-self to constantly think about the object of your desire. I get *why* you'd want to think about your crush all the time—it beats think-ing about basically anything currently going on in the world. Given the choice to think about anti-vaxxers, America's growing iso-lationism, or making out with a hot dude in our huge country house, I'm thinking about making out! It's also just fun and com-forting to imagine a future with someone. It's nice to tell yourself stories in which your life ends up great!

Chances are if you're thinking about your crush that much, you're talking about them all the time, too. This is creepy, yes, but primarily this is boring. Your feelings about any specific hot guy are the least interesting thing about you. *You know this!!* Probably you try to avoid bringing them up. Unfortunately, one of the hall-marks of being obsessively into someone is that you can make anything—*Black Mirror*, the unwritten constitution of the United Kingdom, a video of lemurs attacking a reporter—somehow re-lated to the person you're into.

In a way, when I'm that into someone (which it is my psychic burden to be approximately 90 percent of the time) I get a perverse pleasure from publicly wallowing in my obsession. I am completely whacked out, and I want the world to know! I might be at work, but my mind is on *other things*, namely my fake children, Aoife and Caoimhe Roberson-Chalamet. (Names of my crush have been changed to Timothée Chalamet to protect guys I haven't told yet that I have a crush on them, and also to alert Timothée Chalamet to the fact that I want to have two Irish daughters with him.) I'd talk about one guy so much that even my boss, a very professional person, started saying "Ooh, Timothée" whenever I said "TIMO-THÉE THINKS . . ." I had a mutual friend who specifically was uncomfortable talking about Timothée, but I just couldn't stop myself because I was so obsessed.

Barthes writes in *A Lover's Discourse*: "Love had made him into a social catastrophe, to his delight." After thinking about it, I'm pretty sure Barthes was talking about something totally different from what I'm describing, like when I thought the Georgia O'Keeffe quote "Your life is your art as well as the thing you call your art" was about being a good person, when I later found out it's about, like, organizing your bookshelves by color. But there is something gratifying in being a social catastrophe. I enjoy how my crushes can make me into an objectively insane person who is horrible to hang out with. It's a lot of feelings at once, and even if they express themselves as annoying to other people, it's like: hey, fish are definitely not feeling this! Grass isn't feeling this! I'm a human and [shouts into megaphone] newsflash, dipshits: I've got a crush! My crush is the hottest person in the world, if my boss/friends/Lyft driver saw him they'd know, and in fact here's a photo, come look! By thinking and speaking about him constantly, my love becomes as real in everybody else's mind as it is in mine.

But chances are that if you think about your object of desire too much, you suffocate the real relationship with the weight of the narratives you're creating in your head. You're depriving it of the space to grow and surprise and just exist. Like: I *believe* I could probably act normal after imagining every possible scenario in which a guy and I would kiss for the first time, and whether I'd sleep over after we hooked up, and if I'd actually say yes if he asked to date exclusively, and how our friends would react when we broke up. But it would be a lot easier to be *sure* I'd act normal if I hadn't thought about all those things.

Interesting Topics to Think and Talk About That Are Not Some Dude You Hung Out with Two and a Half Times but Never Kissed

- ◆ Plan a road trip around the American Southwest. Put every destination into Google Maps to waste extra time.
- ◆ Who should have played Young Dumbledore instead of Jude Law, who is not young. (Ben Whishaw.)

- Why Twitter and Facebook protect powerful white men but not Muslims, people of color, or women.
- Should you become Catholic again?
- The fact that Leonardo da Vinci was a notorious procrastinator and finished only, like, fifteen paintings in his whole life. Is success totally arbitrary? Or just really a lot easier for white men even if they have no work ethic?
- Buzz Aldrin has walked on the moon; does this make him an honorary witch?
- A possum that recently broke into a liquor store and got drunk.
- Walt Whitman, I guess? I don't know, man, I wonder if anyone has tagged any new photos of this hot dude on Instagram in the last twelve minutes.

Blurry-Faced Crushes

There's a period, in the beginning of having a crush on somebody, when I can't remember exactly what he looks like. Maybe this is because I often have crushes on men who look very similar, and they kind of blend together in my mind. Maybe it's because I can't stop myself from thinking about them, and science says that memories are altered every time we revisit them. Maybe it's because I have a very specific type of amnesia that is also responsible for me never being able to remember who I lend any of my books to.

I found something akin to this feeling described in Edith Wharton's *The Age of Innocence*. Newland Archer, our protagonist/anti-hero, tells his star-crossed love, Ellen, "Each time you happen to me all over again." This doesn't necessarily mean he literally can't remember what she looks like—though the internet didn't exist and you couldn't scroll through people's media tab on Twitter, so I wouldn't be surprised if nobody in the 1870s remembered what anybody else looked like. But Wharton captured here the more *interesting* part of the blurry-crush experience, where every time I see him I feel anew the intensity of my crush, and in a rush I am reminded of all of the specifics that make him such a fantastic and precise and crushable human. I wish I could imprint the details into my mind but I'm too distracted by him in the moment.

The feeling is more exactly like the episode of *Sex and the City* where Carrie can't remember what Berger looks like, which is what happens when she really likes someone. I don't think I would even notice the phenomenon if I hadn't spent the summer before college renting the DVDs of every season of *SATC* from the Antioch Public Library. Similarly: at least once a day I notice a basement door sidewalk grate and think about the episode where Samantha falls into one. But I sometimes wonder if *Sex and the City* gave me the framework to understand and name this organic thing, or if my performance of dating was created by the show, and the only reason I forget cute guys' faces is because Carrie did it. Just like technology and medicine build on foundations laid by previous generations, I believe the way we think and love are influenced by generations' worth of narratives about how to do those things. I couldn't help but wonder: Do we have free will in dating, or am I always just mimicking something I saw on TV?

Either way, this happened to me a lot with a specific guy I liked, so much that I told him that when we weren't together I could never remember exactly what he looked like, and I was always a little shocked when I saw him again. (We don't kiss anymore, but it still happens. I saw him across a theater looking for his seat recently and gasped so loudly that multiple people turned.) His response to this was very (a) what the hell are you talking about and (b) why are you telling me this. Clearly the man had never seen season five, episode five of *Sex and the City*. I told him it was probably because of how different he looked in glasses, and we moved on.

Sure, Okay

Barthes writes that "we are astonished if we hear of someone's *deciding* to fall in love," but I have often throughout the course of my life suspected that a guy was into me and decided sure, okay, I could be into him as well. It's really NOT HARD to trick yourself into an obsessive thought spiral, and the fact that a person is into you seems as good a reason as any. Biological anthropologist Dr. Helen Fisher describes this in *Anatomy of Love*; she says that we prefer those who like us back because we enjoy feeling that we are likable. When you spend your time worrying that the line between good and evil passes through the heart of every human being EX-

CEPT YOU, a being of PURE EVIL, it's nice to hang with a dude who thinks you are (a) good and (b) hot!

In a way it's nice that I can convince myself to be into anyone. We're all humans, there is something to love in everyone, connection is important to our species, and, at the end of the day, everyone is hot. And maybe part of every romantic relationship is willfully ignoring parts of the other you don't find innately attractive. No one is perfect; there's not some other half of you running around out there who loves all the same music, has the same overly progressive opinions about superhero movies, and who looks like the adult version of your sixth-grade crush. It's an especially essential skill in straight culture: women attracted to men have to selectively ignore the fact that their partner benefits from a culture that oppresses women and that he probably actively participates in that culture in many ways. If you refused to date every man who doesn't want to hear about how Pablo Picasso treated the women in his life, or who thinks the wage gap comes down to lifestyle choices, or who thinks that all of your complaints about sexism can be tedious, there might not be anyone left to date. So in practice, when a man who is otherwise a Good, Hot Ally is dismissive of a feminist point or makes a joke that is kind of fucked up, you file in your head to try to change him later and remind yourself that LA LA LA he is tall and good with kids! I wouldn't marry this guy, but sometimes you just really want to have someone to get sexy drinks with for a couple months!

Deciding to be attracted to someone can help you "practice" love while you're young, to try it without any stakes. Elena, the teenage heroine of Elena Ferrante's *My Brilliant Friend*, refers to her boyfriend as a "useful phantom." And, sure, if both parties are on board with a certain amount of laissez-faire who-gives-a-shit distance, then I guess knock yourself out, teens. Though there are probably better ways to use your time? Like digging a very, very deep hole for fun, getting stuck in the hole, and setting off a national media circus?

But convincing yourself to like someone just because they like you seems to be an unsteady foundation for anything real. I heard someone somewhere say (honestly I probably read this in *Elle Girl* when I was eleven) that when listing what you love about someone, it's not real love if all your answers are about you: "They make me feel hot." "I love how much they pay attention to me." "They told me that to respect my privacy they won't read this book but also that they know it is brilliant."

"Sure, okay" is even LESS healthy when—as has happened to me—you're not even totally convinced the guy is into you, and, upon further investigation, he's not. Says Barthes: "I thought I was suffering from not being loved, and yet it is because I thought I was loved that I was suffering; I lived in the complication of supposing myself simultaneously loved and abandoned." Like: *as an act of charity* I decided to become obsessed with you when I could tell you were secretly and shyly into me. Now it turns out you just had no friends in a new city and I'm waking up my male roommate to analyze every single text you send me??? I'm very over the phenomena of having mental breakdowns when guys I am NOT EVEN INTO haven't texted me.

Compounding that problem is my belief that everyone is

secretly in love with me. We're all familiar with the belief, or posture, that one is inherently unlovable; there are so many "sad single girl" characters on TV and in life. When I first moved to New York City, a coworker told me I was leaning too hard into the sad single girl character, even though I was legitimately just a single girl! Who wasn't even particularly sad about it! My guess is that the suspicion that everyone is secretly in love you with has something to do with our current self-esteem culture, where well-meaning magazines and teachers combat a society that continuously beats women down by telling us that we should instead feel all the time like we are the greatest ever. It's a nice message, but without an examination of how and why women are oppressed, it's confusing. It lends itself to simultaneously believing that everyone is in love with me AND that I am inherently unlovable. (Instead, perhaps, we should just be gentle and loving with ourselves, without having to believe we are immortal heroes.) When you're certain everyone is in love with you, you can decide you're in love with anyone. Which is how I have ended up with a number of crushes greater than the population of Iceland.

Man Management

When you are casually talking to/texting/hanging out with/kissing/aspiring to IRL meet multiple men, it can be very difficult to keep track of it all. Maybe back in the day when written language wasn't invented and everybody had to just remember *The Iliad*, human memory was better and they could have remembered what the status was with each of their crushes. But now the internet exists, and even back when I was in high school my teachers gave up on asking us to memorize things because "in real life you can just google it." Because of this, I cannot even remember who all of my crushes ARE at any given moment.

There are probably many ways to deal with this. You could change your crushes' names in your phone from "Graham From Party" to "Graham From Kissing" to "Graham Do Not Text." You could invent a crush-tracking app, like a period app but for crushes. (If this does not already exist, I will trade this idea for ten thousand dollars or my own basic-cable sitcom.) My very brilliant friend Fran created a secret Facebook group for her crushes. But the method I personally use is a (private!) Google Docs spreadsheet.

In a moment of desperation in spring 2016, to prove to myself that I did know hot men, I made a very simple spreadsheet of men and my status with them. This is normal because dating is labor invented to keep women busy, and if I'm going to have a side job I might as well use the Google Docs acumen I list on my freaking résumé. Unfortunately this spreadsheet just made me depressed. Under "STATUS" it listed "Doesn't want to hang," "Doesn't want to hang," "Doesn't want to hang," "???," "Have never met this person," "Ten-year plan," another "???," and finally "Explicitly doesn't like me."

I deleted it. Then, in another moment of desperation months later, I created a very similar spreadsheet, this time ranking the men by plausibility that I would ever kiss them (three of the bottom four were "10-year plan"). But magically, the same night that I made the spreadsheet, I boned the guy in the top slot! Life is meaningless and nothing happens for a reason.

Objectively, I do think it would be useful to have a list of all the men I think are hot, *if* I were then willing to put in effort to pursue these men. Instead, I like to withdraw into myself and my writing and just "wait for the magic to happen." The fun and exciting thing about doing nothing is that it will never work, because human relationships are not magic. But I have convinced myself that if somehow it *does* work, the fact that I did not pursue it will mean that it is more pure. Having a filing system for men I'm trying to form a deep emotional connection with makes me feel sociopathic in an unsexy way (though, in a smaller way, these documents also feel like art objects that I expect to be included to pad out a boring room in my MoMA PS1 retrospective). So until I can trap all my crushes on an island in a rom-com version of *Lord of the Flies*, I'm stuck texting whoever's top of mind. Which isn't too bad a system.

Categories for My Crush-Tracking App

NAME
A: Will
B: Other

AGE
A: Year younger
B: Year older
C: Twenty-nine and talks exclusively about feeling
   weird about it
D: Could honestly be forty for all I know

SIGN
A: Gemini
B: Virgo
C: Cancer
D: One of the good ones

LAST INTERACTION
A: Mutual friend's birthday dinner nine months
   ago
B: Took him to a cool work event to impress
   him
C: Literally cannot remember
D: We're boinking

IS HE INTO ME?
A: Optimistically . . . neutral
B: No???
C: I'm convinced (so maybe)
D: LOL yes, we're . . . and I can't believe you're
   making me use this word again . . . boinking

AM I INTO HIM?

A: Unfortunately

B: Yes, if memory serves

C: There exists a future in which I could be

D: Yes, to the exact degree we're already (sighs for ten full minutes) boinking

HAS HE DATED YOUR FRIENDS?

A: No

B: Yes, but they're fine

C: Uhhh, I wouldn't call her a "friend"

D: I had never even heard of this guy before I met him, which is 75 percent of the attraction

HAVE YOU HEARD RUMORS THAT HE HAS BEEN BAD TO OTHER WOMEN?

A: No

[this is the only option; my app isn't here to enable anyone]

ARE YOU TELLING OTHER PEOPLE?

A: No

B: Mentioned offhand to friends

C: Gave friends play-by-play of every text he's ever sent me

D: Told parents I know someone with his first name (very serious)

NEXT MOVES

A: Orchestrate group hang

B: Drinks

C: Figure out if he's still living in Costa Rica

D: Continue boinking

2

FLIRTING

Signals

Flirting is a game of giving and interpreting signals. Deducing the meanings of these "clues" sustains entire rom-coms and brunches.

To be respectful about pursuing someone in a way that ultimately involves bodies and/or hearts, you do want to start small and gently and become progressively more frank as you get the consent of the other person. (This, I believe, is the point of Dave Chappelle's "Take It to the Next Level" speech in *You've Got Mail*, a movie that so wastes his genius it has shaken my faith in Nora Ephron, moviemaking, art, and the arc of mankind.) You have to be respectful and feel people out! You can't just bop someone on the head with your dinger fresh out the gate! That's not a flirt!

But it can be *extremely hard* to decipher signals at the early stages because they are either imperceptibly subtle or, more often (for me at least), because they are nonexistent and exist only in your head. And, to be fair, we are very motivated to imagine signals where they don't exist. It is easy to feel, in this society that is so aggro about pushing coupledom and about basing women's worth on their fuckability, that the existence of any person who is not attracted to you in some way demeans you. Or perhaps you view yourself as the protagonist of your story and every story and it only makes narrative sense that this person MUST be into you. (See: the pilot of *Seinfeld*.)

Historically, I have gotten poor peer reviews in the whole "signal" area. I have been accused of "playing Hard To Understand." I have been accused of being "incapable of giving or receiving signals."

Certainly, in retrospect, there have been many times when I, a timid flower who had never kissed anyone, thought I was giving signals when in fact I was standing completely motionless, eyes averted. Like the time I read Jonathan Franzen's *The Corrections* in a hot guy's direction while standing in line for an improv show. These things feel meaningful to me because of what I am feeling inside. But probably zero percent of my flirts registered with their intended targets for the first ten years of my flirting career.

But even flirts that don't exist entirely in your head can be lost on men, specifically. I don't say this just because numerous scientific studies have shown that all women are psychic and can move objects with their minds. And I'm not just saying this because dudes are always drinking IPAs, which numerous scientific studies at our nation's most respected research universities have shown mutes your psychic ability. I say this because women are socialized to pay attention to and to cater to people's emotions in a way that men are not. This is why there are six seasons of *Sex and the City* and why I will die by walking into a manhole while group texting five women about whether a guy was giving me signals: women are trained to read men's thoughts! We analyzed microexpressions for millennia before it became a cool thing for Martin Short to do on *Law & Order: SVU*! Society has relegated us to emotional labor, and while it is super fucked up, we have gotten really good at it! So while I'm over here analyzing a guy's blinks to prove he's in love with me, men don't even see that there is any data to be sorted through. To them, subtle emotions are like the cipher on the back of the Declaration of Independence, and they don't even know they need to put lemon juice on it and stick it in the oven at Jon Voight's house. Hell, they probably don't even know they need to steal the Declaration of Independence in the first place!

I do think, with age and experience and growing courage and belief in myself, I have improved at giving signals, at making my interest known. I think I've gotten marginally better at knowing what touches are specifically flirty and at long silences that involve looking at lips. I have improved less at knowing when a guy is interested in me. I still spend a lot of time analyzing men's words and actions and [extremely Ursula voice] body language, both because this is the patriarchal water I swim in and because, apparently, I like to do it!

It's kind of disturbing how thrilling the uncertainty of early flirting can be. Kate Bolick writes in *Spinster* that in the olden days, girls would stay hidden until age eighteen, then get engaged within a year of debuting in society. That one year was essentially the one exciting year of a woman's life. It's also the stage of romance we see most often depicted in fairy tales, rom-coms, Jane Austen novels, and rom-coms loosely based on Jane Austen novels: two people meet, flirt, and in the final scene decide they're both explicitly into one another. There's a double wedding, Hugh Grant throws coins on everyone's head, and for all we know they drive into a pond and immediately drown.

It is very possible that I (subconsciously?) think that love is only exciting in the beginning, that once you find a partner you're basically just two skeletons waiting around to die. (Or at least the boring/domestic/house-bound/nagging "wife" is.) As soon as I establish that one guy is interested in me and we begin to see each other regularly, I immediately become fixated on flirting with someone else whose interest is less sure. Like one of Don Draper's exes tells him: "You only like the beginnings of things." I'm a fan of the middle of things, too, in the unofficial capacity I've experienced them—it's nice to have emotional support, a reliable date, someone whose family you can ask after and whose life you can try in your own way to improve—but that kind of romantic attraction feels to me almost closer to friendship. It's great and it's nourishing, but it's not fun in the way that the beginnings of things are, when living your own love life feels like watching an episode of *Game of Thrones* (extremely anxious in a good way, constantly formulating fan theories). And I like the early stages of flirtations because I guess I'm just addicted to the thought of always being on the verge of being validated by a new person! Getting a new crush to kiss you is like proving that someone who knows how to skateboard and can build furniture thinks that YOU, specifically, have worth! Even though you (I) can only skateboard in a straight line and building an IKEA dresser took you (me) eight hours, most of which were spent eating chocolate-covered pomegranate seeds!

Because young people are waiting longer to permanently pair off, because it's normal to go through many partners, I sometimes wonder if—by acting "chill" and becoming okay with relationships not lasting for long—I've become too addicted to the beginning of things to pick one person and settle down. Which, if it just meant I never ended up with a husband, who cares. I am only too happy to live my best single Martha Stewart life, hawking books about flower arranging and taking subpar pictures of icebergs on my iPhone X well into my golden years. BUT I think that the excitement that comes from the beginning of things comes mostly at the expense of the other person (not in the "sleeping with a billion hot new people" way that we associate with men and often label as exploitative, though it doesn't necessarily need to be either of those things—the excitement I'm talking about comes from the emotional uncertainty and drama). The stage of a relationship during which you're analyzing signals is so much more about you than it is about your crush; they're basically an idea of a person, someone you've mapped your assumptions onto. If these boys want to be *excluded from this narrative,* this is not fun for them. Boys do not ask to be in my head and my tweets twenty-four/seven! Obviously there's always some level of uncertainty when you're first figuring out how you and another person feel about each other, but I don't want to relish in the deciphering that happens in the beginning of a relationship so much that it becomes the end in itself.

My current kick is to JUST SAY HOW I FEEL. It is very scary, and I manage to do it between 5 and 25 percent of the time.

Text Interpretation

Barthes wrote about agonizing over signals: "Signs are not proofs, since anyone can produce false or ambiguous signs. Hence one falls back, paradoxically, on the omnipotence of language [. . .] I shall receive every word from my other as a sign of truth; and when I speak, I shall not doubt that he, too, receives what I say as the truth." But (not to straight-up quote freshman-year-of-college, paper-is-due-at-ten-A.M.-and-it's-three-A.M. me), language is insufficient to express the enormity and complexity of human thought and feeling, so while speaking honestly is definitely advisable, it's not going to solve dating. If there's one thing I learned studying English for four years, it's that you can interpret any text any way you want, and if you interpret it through a Marxist lens you will get an A.

If we, like Barthes, are to fall back on the omnipotence of language, texting would seem the ideal way to express romantic feelings. It's almost all words! And then also emojis, probably selfies if you're doing it right, and maybe gifs if you are more organized than I am. But obviously, hello: texting is no respite from agonizing and analyzing.

To be clear up top, I should say that my strong feeling is that if you need to analyze someone's texts to find a reading that means this person is into you, then they aren't into you. At best, they MAYBE are or they MAYBE will be in the future, but even if either is true, you have better things to do with your time, like wash your bras or run for local office. People who are into you just ask you to hang out, or say yes when you ask them to hang out. Sometimes they just show up where they know you'll be, in a respectful and hot way.

But, again, I am someone whose higher education consisted of four years reading *The Great Gatsby* through every conceivable lens. I spent the most formative years of my life learning that you can interpret books/poems/any group of words you want in five hundred thousand different ways, because there are five hundred thousand different schools of literary theory. For example, here are a few I remember:

There's close reading, which is basically what we were taught in high school, although of course all I can remember from high school is every detail of every interaction I ever had with the hot dude who was captain of our football team. Close reading is the thing where you view a text as closed off from outside information and just really dig into ~~the words~~. It was invented by the New Critics, which consisted of Robert Penn Warren and a bunch of other white dudes from the South. So while I love close reading, I am VERY SUSPICIOUS OF IT and fully expect to have to someday disown it following troubling allegations about its behavior toward women.

There's biographical reading, in which you consider the author's life, but this is considered BAD. There's considering the author's intentions, which is apparently WORSE, because WHO CARES and AUTHORS ARE MORONS. I don't know what these techniques are actually called because I stuck mostly to the How-Does-This-Relate-to-*Twilight* reading, which I am thrilled to say once got me an A-minus on a paper about *Wuthering Heights* and absolutely no other A's. There's semiotics? Which I have heard of.

But I have no idea what it is. There's psychoanalytic literary criticism, a field which is now, I believe, practiced only by people who specifically are trying to be annoying and entirely miss the point. There's deconstruction, which I cannot remember anything about other than the fact that it made me extremely nauseous and confused. My opinion on all schools of literary thought is now: Oh, hundreds of years of white men thought about this subject? Let me throw all of that out the window and do whatever I feel like!

So, with all of this training poured into me by some of our nation's most respected intellectuals and scholars, I now possess the ability to analyze any text in such a way that it irrefutably means the guy is into me, or hates me. This skill was pointed out to me by my friend Jonah, who is like a therapist who I do not pay and who is tasked with coordinating production elements for a late-night show while diagnosing me, and who said: "It's almost amazing how you can turn innocuous things I say into insults or compliments." And I was like: oh, this is why I paid five hundred trillion dollars to go to school.

Using My Four-Year College English Degree to Close-Read Texts from Men

TEXT:

Me: What Pokémon should I date???????

Him: Dugtrio

INTERPRETATION:
You, Blythe, deserve three boyfriends.

TEXT:
[he is trying out the iOS feature where you can draw and sends an arch]
Him: That's a marriage arch
[he draws a circle]
Him: This is a ring
INTERPRETATION:
We just met tonight but I already know that I want to spend the rest of my life with you.

TEXT:
[a photo of a beer I'd left unfinished at a party]
Him: I'm drinking your beer by the by
INTERPRETATION:
I want my mouth where your mouth has been.

TEXT:
Me: Text me if you want to get a drink.
Him: I want to!
INTERPRETATION:
I have never felt anything in my life as strongly as I feel the desire to get a drink with you; hence, the exclamation point sent by me, a man.

TEXT:

Him: I reckon I'd strut with 20% more sass if I was
    called Blythe.

INTERPRETATION:

Let's have five hundred children and name them
all Blythe.

TEXT:

Him: I think you need an official commendation for
    the strength of your venmo emojis as they
    were unusually precise

INTERPRETATION:

I have an enormous respect for your mind and
believe you may be one of the creative geniuses
of our generation.

TEXT:

[a gif he made of two photos of us]

INTERPRETATION:

I have memorialized our meeting in art.

*Note: Now that I am rereading these texts I am once again absolutely
certain every single one of these were extremely bold and obvious
flirts.*

I Know It When I See It

It is very hard to definitively prove that someone was flirting with you. I discovered this after a man who had been flirting with me for three months told me that he had never once flirted with me in his whole life, and I had to try to explain to him why I knew he was wrong.

Here's the backstory: the first time we hung out, he accompanied me to the witch store to buy candles and a literal cauldron. Then we walked around Tompkins Square Park looking at small dogs until we stumbled on a bar with sidewalk seating, where we traded romantic histories and I read his tarot. For me, I was like: This guy wants to marry me. Who else would consent to get their tarot read in public the first time we hang out? Who else would hang out with me during the worst stage of my Acne Crisis of 2016? But matters were complicated by the fact that I waited three months to try to kiss him, because I am a coward and also we worked together. Hence, the disagreement: Had we been flirting?

Things he had done which I thought were flirting:

- Taking online state trivia quizzes when I asked him to.
- Coming into my office every day and just "chilling."
- Doing a crossword with me in a quiet bar lit only by candles at one in the morning.

◆ Listening to me when I spoke. (It is insane how
   little men have to do to be considered hot.)
◆ Patting me awkwardly on the head.

Admittedly that last one is weak, but in the moment it felt
charged, if a head pat can ever be considered "charged."

In the majority opinion on the case Jacobellis v. Ohio, which
decided whether the Louis Malle film *The Lovers* was obscene, Su-
preme Court Justice Potter Stewart wrote, "I shall not today attempt further to define the kinds of material I understand to be
embraced within that shorthand description, and perhaps I could
never succeed in intelligibly doing so. But I know it when I see it,
and the motion picture involved in this case is not that." People
didn't read Stewart's opinion and say, "*I know it when I see it*?! Wow,
what an idiot, try to use your words, didn't you go to Yale?" Generally they were like, "Honestly . . . yeah," and applauded his ruling
for being realistic and candid. (Or so says my brother, who went
to law school. My entire legal training consists of watching every
episode of *The Good Wife*, which I truly consider equivalent to a
law degree.)

So I had a hard time explaining to this guy why I knew he was
100 percent flirting with me, but I was saved from feeling crazy
and desperate by the fact that everyone I work with agreed with
me. There was a rumor that this guy and I were secretly dating. A
coworker felt hurt that I hadn't confided this nonexistent relationship to her, after some dude I don't even know who worked in a
totally different department casually mentioned it to her. None of

my work friends could conclusively prove the existence of flirting either, but, at some point, We All Saw It and Knew It.

NONE OF THIS is to say that you can touch, kiss, or even act flirty to someone who says they aren't flirting with you! Consent is essential, and when someone tells you that this isn't that kind of situation, you absolutely cannot "argue" the point. (And, like, what, are you going to argue so well that you get married?!) Let's also remember that gender is important here. Sexual predators are usually men. Women are certainly capable of sexually harassing men, but we haven't been oppressing men for millennia, allowing us to leverage our power in the workplace and in the public eye to enable that harassment. Meanwhile, I think that to save his male pride or whatever, this guy denied flirting with me in a way that made me feel crazy—in a "relationship crazy" way that women are often pigeonholed and made to feel less than. (For the record, he has read this chapter and still says he wasn't flirting with me. Is there any such thing as truth?)

Men I Thought Were Flirting with Me, and Why

A disclaimer: All names have been changed, and just because I thought these men were flirting with me doesn't mean I was in love with them. It makes sense that a lot of people would be flirting with me, since I am hitting all four quadrants: (1) Hot (I have good hair and good boobs), (2) Smart (I know about recent scientific developments), (3) Funny (I have studied improv in both New York AND Chicago at a total cost of one million dollars), and (4): Rude.

MATTHEW

Matthew and I were seeing a movie, and to kill time during the previews I was like, "Oh, you studied film theory, you should make me a list of movies for me to watch." He sent me an email that night with NINETY-NINE MOVIES on it (I think; it is hard to count that high) and the message "Your eyes and mind can thank me later." I was like: "Oh, this guy is in love with me," so I spent the next year deciding I was in love with him. Later I asked him if he was flirting with me and he said he was "just enthusiastic about movies."

JAMES

For a period of about two months, James faved all of my tweets. In 2018 this would make sense, but this was in 2014, when my tweets were, like, fine. I asked James if he was flirting with me and he said, "No, I'm just on my phone a lot."

MICHAEL

Watched all 119 minutes of *You've Got Mail* with me.

BENJAMIN

I met Benjamin on a stormy night in 2015, just before I saw a midnight screening of the Minions movie. He leaned out of a shadowy corner of a bar and asked me if I was the Blythe Roberson who wrote the David Foster Wallace article for *Splitsider*. I had, THREE YEARS EARLIER. If that isn't a flirt, please put me in a boat and push me into the ocean to die. Benjamin and I later made plans to get drinks, but he blew me off to go on a date with a twenty-three-year-old blond girl with a six-pack.

LUKE

Gave me a really long hug. That sounds normal, but if you were there you would have been like [checks watch], "Whaaaaaat is going on."

LACHLAN

Sent me a picture of a bunch of foods and said, "These are my foods so you know my foods."

MITCHELL

Rented a car to pick me up for a pizza dinner in a car. Men are sociopaths.

DYLAN

Saw me do a comedy routine about men I thought were flirting with me, and ever since has constantly asked if I think he's flirting with me. HE IS.

> NOTE: There is almost no correlation between people I thought were flirting with me and those who actually were. I have since learned that the only real flirts are (a) not leaving, (b) talking about bread, (c) making weird eyes, and (d) making a real effort to spend time with me. The last one is theoretical as no one in human history has yet done it.

Digital Flirting

Digital flirting seems less real, and therefore lower stakes, than real-life flirting. This is wrong, obviously: the internet *is* real, and soon all of our brains will live inside of it, and when we die our consciousnesses will be uploaded into incredibly sleek refrigerators.

In fact, digital flirting is in a sense more real than in-person banter, because it leaves a paper trail. Your texts and Gchats and DMs are there for the searching, in case you're in the mood to embarrass yourself or write a tell-all. And I've been digital flirting for about as long as I've been flirting at all—the first time I ever told a guy I liked him it was via AIM, and the first time a guy ever told me he had feelings for me it was also via AIM. Of course, it took about fifteen minutes to figure out he had said he had feelings for me, because he was so bad at typing.

Since you get to avoid the risk of being rejected to your face, flirting via your devices is the perfect type of flirting not just for young people who live online but for romantic cowards of any age. It's a good way to build up to real-life flirts.

Some digital flirts to get you started:

Following your crush on social media: This is an admission that, at least in the second that you clicked that "follow" button, you were thinking about your crush on your own time. Maybe you believe this barely counts as a flirt, but if you are very closed off to being vulnerable in any way or if your crush is very hot this can be scary! I remember exactly where I was when one of my old crushes followed me on Twitter. I sat in a café for half an hour afterward thinking about my beautiful new Twitter follower. I go back there sometimes to relive the high! I saw Patti Smith at that café once, but it remains "the café where my crush followed me on Twitter and also secondarily where I saw Patti Smith." One time I Facebook friend requested a crush and he used that as an excuse to text me; I almost fainted. Conversely! I once followed on Twitter someone I had hooked up with, and he did not follow me back until I directly told him that he had an obligation to. If you frenched someone THAT WEEK then you have to follow them back on Twitter! It's protocol!

Follow someone on Twitter while you are sitting next to them: An admission that this person will continue to exist, outside of this bar.

Scroll through someone's entire Instagram while sitting next to them: A very fun flirt that I stumbled into is, when out with someone for the first time, scrolling back through YEARS of their Instagram, laughing and faving and telling them which posts you like. The guy I did this to called it "I can't believe you're doing this" and "This is my worst nightmare" and "I'm going to the bathroom until you're done."

Liking the same content on multiple platforms: Someone tweets a link to a music video their band just released. Maybe it's good, or maybe you just want to support your friend, or maybe because all your friends are geniuses it is both, so: you fave the tweet. VERY NORMAL AND GOOD MOVE. You have paid your friend in notifications and serotonin in exchange for their art and friendship. BUT: if they post the video on Facebook and Instagram, too, and you like those, and maybe even post a comment? Maybe even TEXT THEM ALSO? In my opinion, that's a digital flirt. I know that there are people in the world who are just "supportive," but I will never like your content on more than one platform unless I am interested in holding hands and staring deeply into your eyes.

Fave a recent tweet, wait half an hour, and fave a tweet from six months ago: I have never done this, but it was recently done to me and it. Is. Chilling. This is the Twitter equivalent of a horse's head in a bed, I think, though much like Meg Ryan in *You've Got Mail* I do not and cannot give a shit about *The Godfather*. But, man, did I feel seen. This dude had paid attention to me in a very intense way, and like the nun tells Lady Bird in *Lady Bird*, love and attention are the same thing.

Good Analog Flirts That Work

Paying attention. According to journalist Ann Friedman, "Flirting is undivided attention." For men, all you need to do in order to be attractive is pay attention when a woman talks. For women, the bar is much higher.

Making weird eyes. There's something that happens to people's eyes right when they're trying to kiss you. They're unfocused, or maybe way too focused? Without context, it looks like they're fixing to kill you. In context: solid flirt.

Refusing to leave. A great, low-effort, low-bravery flirt that gets the point across. You may feel uncomfortable, but just sticking around until everyone other than your crush leaves the party or the bar significantly raises your chances of smooching. I know of at least one years-long relationship that started this way. Heck, if you stay at my party until three in the morning, I'll make out with you just to reward your effort.

Saying your crush's full name to their face. I have no idea why this works. It's a spell? We live in a narcissistic culture? It's super weird, and when hot people are weird it's a flirt?

Sitting your crush down, asking their zodiac sign, and then reading them your full two-page sextrology compatibility profile. I have never felt more powerful than when doing this.

Showing them your Twitter drafts. Extremely vulnerable!

Saying nothing. "Talking" is something people do with their mouths when they are too nervous to kiss you. Do not encourage them! Refuse to respond; they'll get the idea.

Sending them One Direction songs. I often ask dudes to watch *You've Got Mail* with me or to listen to the acoustic version of "Steal My Girl" because I genuinely love these things but I know they are not most guys' jam. This is a test to see if these guys are "game." I have a lot of bad opinions. Can they be nice to me for one fucking second? As John Waters said, if you go home with somebody and they can't be nice to you for one fucking second, don't fuck them.

Bad Flirts That Do Not Work

I love these flirts, and while they may not work, committing to experimental flirts is its own reward.

Standing completely still and not doing anything. This flirt works at the *end* of a date, to get someone to kiss you. It does *not* work to catch someone's eye and get them to ask you on a date.

Chanting "walk me home" to convince them to walk you home. They will walk you home, and then they will immediately call an Uber.

Showing them all the stuff in your purse. It is extremely obvious that this is a bad and boring flirt, but it is encoded in my DNA to do this. I guess I subconsciously picked it up from *The Breakfast Club*? It has never ended in anything other than me apologizing for not having anything interesting in my purse.

Talking about your amazing cosmic compatibility with your friend Fran. When the guy asks you what his and yours is together, you say: "Very bad."

Saying "who??" when comedy boys talk about Simon Rich. It seems like it would be a hilarious troll, but the comedy boys just get very genuinely confused.

Forcing guys into extracurricular activities and then doing all their work for them. I did this a lot in high school, and while I never got a boyfriend, I did single-handedly get three guys into college.

Correcting someone's grammar. Guys do this to me constantly, and in order to stay calm I choose to view it as a flirt. But even then: it is not a good flirt.

Texting them that you're across the street from their apartment. Someone once did this to me, and while I appreciated where his head was at, I have a schedule. I make it three weeks in advance.

Scheming. Elaborate plans to ensnare men's affection never work (see: the entire plot of *My Best Friend's Wedding*), but it is fun to scheme because it is so truly stupid. And when you are at once very type A and very sure that you are not sexy enough to naturally have people want to kiss you, *Ocean's 11*-ing your way to affection seems like a way to assert some control over the situation. I've gone on vacation to a dude's city so that we could casually hang out and fall in love (we didn't). I've tried to get a guy to do the "Thirty-Six Questions That Lead to Love" thing (we started making out before I could enact the plan). Scheming: when just not talking and blinking in a sexy way *would* work, but you have a lot of time on your hands, so why not.

Stealing

This section encompasses all the ways in which, in the beginning of a flirtation or relationship, you end up with an object belonging to the other. I call this section "stealing" simply because I live for drama.

Stealing something from your crush is a huge flirt, and historically one of my favorites. The platonic ideal of this flirt is when, in high school, my crush loaned me his hoodie when I was cold at some manner of outdoor sporting event (the athletic details of which I was surely even then actively erasing from my mind). The flirt part comes in when I . . . just didn't give the hoodie back.

Stealing as a flirt feels very "high school" to me, maybe because it was my main move in high school, or maybe because it involves feeling mischievous, or maybe because you're externalizing your feelings onto a dumb hoodie and turning that hoodie into physical proof of your connection with your crush. It's tangible evidence that they prefer you *don't* die of hypothermia! That they trust you to not get yourself covered in mustard in the next several hours! That they are okay with people seeing your body covered in a hoodie screen-printed with their last name and football jersey number!

Roland Barthes (daddy) wrote that "The gift is contact, sensuality: you will be touching what I have touched, a third skin unites us. I give X a scarf and he wears it: X *gives* me the fact of wearing it." Okay. Like . . . no dudes have ever *gifted* me an article of clothing, presumably because I have not tricked any of them well enough. But it's almost more intense when they lend you/let you steal their hoodie. They're giving you the gift of the hoodie and also the gift of you wearing the hoodie. They're letting you touch this thing that they have touched. The gift of the third skin is exponentially more significant than the gift of not being chilly at a field hockey (??) regional championship game.

And though this is a "high school" flirt, it's high school in the sugary and fun and "remember when I had emotions??" way: I endorse it.

Usually back then, and exclusively (I think) now, I wasn't actually practicing nonconsensual theft. I was only comfortable truly stealing things from friends who I wasn't agonizing about wanting to kiss. When it came to my crushes, I was just not really in a rush to give these hoodies back. But I loved to have these objects for as long as politely possible and to pretend that I would have them forever. I'm a dragon under a mountain, sleeping on its pile of gold, except instead of gold it's hoodies from my crushes.

The exact opposite of stealing is when you leave something of yours at a man's place. A friend of mine says she used to leave hair ties and bobby pins at men's apartments, things she didn't need back that still left a mark. It sent a message that no matter how "casual" both parties were going to be about the liaison, my friend had in fact EXISTED. I would not be surprised if a similar motivation led to Tayl*r Sw*ft's scarf ending up at Maggie Gyllenhaal's house for all of eternity. When you're as rich as Taylor Swift, a scarf is like a hair tie to you: disposable.

I—a lazy person incapable of plotting and also incapable of remembering almost anything—never leave anything at a guy's house on purpose. With me it's always a case of a Cinderella-type accident, if Cinderella specifically said, "I'm not going to forget this shoe," and then immediately did. An example: I once took off a necklace while hooking up with a guy. "Do not let me forget this necklace!" I said. Two days later, I got a Facebook message of a picture of the necklace. "Did you even realize?"—him.

I did not PLAN to leave it there so that I'd have to see this guy again, but if I had wanted to I could not have planned it better. "Now how in the world am I gonna get this necklace back?" I asked. He answered: "My roommate has a drone." (Everyone I sleep with is a comedian.) Eventually we ended up doing the necklace exchange at a bar in convenient proximity to his apartment [insert sunglasses emoji]. I could have continued "forgetting" the necklace at his place indefinitely, and if I had, this dude and I would very probably be married by now.

All of this stealing and forgetting feels very gender-specific to me, in that I and my friends have not observed it happening in the reverse. Men don't "accidentally" leave small things at my apartment. Often in the dead of winter they suspect they've left their jackets at my place, something which I cannot imagine going more than half a block without noticing I'm missing, but it never turns out that they have. Some men have forcibly loaned their Thomas Pynchon novels to women I know, but this has never happened to me, perhaps because men are intimidated by my *Crying of Lot 49* tattoo—a thigh piece of a trash can that says "This is where *The Crying of Lot 49* belongs: in the trash (I hate this book)." Have men stolen things from me? I believe that many have stolen books that I've loaned them, but I cannot remember which men have which book, so I can't prove it and I can't get my books back. (If you are reading this and we have kissed and you haven't already sued me for defamation of character—please give me back my copy of *The Love Affairs of Nathaniel P.*! There are other, newer men I need to lend it to!) But generally, I think men steal less, maybe because it's not as cute for the person with all the structural power to steal from the person with less. Or maybe men just don't have an evolutionary need to incrementally close the pay gap through the theft of clothing items.

Touching

I'm sitting on a couch in a crowded bar, talking to a friend who I've known for a handful of months. When I met this guy, I was like, "Whoa, who's Hallie's hot friend??!" but he had a girlfriend at the time. He no longer has a girlfriend. The bar I'm in is super loud and there's a live band playing, presumably to punish me, so I lean in to hear this hot friend talk about an old dude named Cletus who haunts the mountains of central Virginia. And then all of a sudden hot friend and I are holding hands. And I instantly realize: Oh, I'm gonna sleep with this guy.

Okay, that last bit was not true for me. I was less confident back when this happened, and the only time in my life when I have instantly and correctly known that I was gonna sleep with some guy was when a guy asked me, "What are some good One Direction songs?" At the time that this happened, when other people at the bar asked me if I was dating hand-touching guy, I was very flustered and confused, and when we hooked up three months later I considered it extremely out of the blue. But honestly: touching is the most basic flirt. It is a gentle preview of what's to come (high-fiving while naked), creating the atmosphere without really containing any of the meaningful content, like a "Next week on *Mad Men*" teaser.

When talking about touching, apparently and unfortunately it is necessary to start by saying it is hugely inappropriate to touch people who do not want to be touched. As society remembers for a roughly twelve-week period every twenty-five years, touching people who do not want to be touched is sexual harassment. Sometimes it is sexual assault. It is very serious and it fucks up people's lives. This is not the book that you should be reading if you're all of a sudden trying to cram for your "how not to sexually terrorize people" exam, but here are some general tips on how to respect other people's boundaries and ownership of their bodies.

NUMBER ONE: Do not touch someone sexually for the first time outside of a context where you are both on the same page about exploring the possibility of holding hands. So like: A date. A party. This rule means you should NOT be touching people in: A business meeting. On the subway. At school. It's not hard; use your common sense and discretion. Unless you are a white man, in which case your common sense has been warped by centuries of society telling you that you are in charge of everything. White men should probably talk this all out with a female friend first. Then pay her for her emotional labor. Pay her for her previous emotional labor, with interest! What I'm saying is straight, cis white men should pay every woman they know twenty thousand dollars.

NUMBER TWO: As mentioned in the "signals" section, flirting has levels that you need to build up to so that you're not just sticking your dinger in someone's ear right off the bat. This is extremely important when it comes to touching—you need to make sure that nonthreatening touches are being received and allowed before moving up to more sensitive touching. Touching my elbow is a lot less sexual than tenderly touching my wrist tattoo and asking me what the meaning behind it is. (The meaning behind all my tattoos is: I got this so that men would touch me in a flirty way and ask me what it means.) Touching someone's knee, as Ellen Olenska does to Newland Archer in a pivotal scene in *The Age of Innocence*, may have basically been hardcore porn back then but is definitely not as flirty/sexual/intense as touching someone's upper thigh. This is . . . obvious. Be a respectful flirter.

NUMBER THREE: In comedy, there's a concept called "punching up." This basically means that you always have to be sure that your jokes are aimed at people with more power than you, because making fun of the weak and the suffering and the powerless is not funny and it's just not kind. You always have to consider your privilege and your targets' privilege when making a joke. Similarly, you need to consider your privilege and your crush's privilege when flirting. If you're an older white male executive at work asking out a young female intern, you have a lot of structural power over her that can make it difficult for her to say no, even if she wants to. You carelessly touching this girl just because you feel like it can fuck up the entire trajectory of her career. You have the whole history of oppression on your side! So stop and think for five fucking milliseconds! If you're gonna take big flirting risks, make sure you're flirting up. Don't use your structural power to put less privileged people in uncomfortable positions. OKAY, JESUS CHRIST, THANK YOU.

Once you are positive that you are not doing anything nonconsensual: touch is very important! It's not just important for flirting and romance and sex. It's just generally important for healthy human psychology. We are built to need and to be comforted by touch, from our friends and our partners and our family. The psychologist Harry Harlow proved this through a series of experiments in which he really emotionally fucked up a bunch of infant rhesus monkeys. (I learned about this as a senior in high school and have been furious every single day ever since.) Harlow took baby monkeys away from their mothers and gave them imitation monkey moms. Some of the fake mothers were covered in terry cloth that simulated touch. Others were made of wood and wire and not only lacked the ability to provide comfort from touch but also looked terrifying. Unsurprisingly, the infant rhesus monkeys who were given wire moms became extremely emotionally disturbed. The morals of this story: Harry Harlow is a true villain, and touch is very important.

To quote Ursula, the heroine of *The Little Mermaid*: "Don't underestimate the importance of body language." (Ursula is the heroine of *The Little Mermaid* because she has a cool witch aesthetic, she is unapologetic about her unruly body, and her main goal in life is to unseat the white male king.)

I have a fascinating scientific fact to tell you about consensual flirty touching. Due to the cultural narrative that men should "make the first move," you may believe that men are the ones who initiate flirty touching. But, as Dr. Helen Fisher tells us in *The Anatomy of Love*, that is not true! Fisher says that American women generally make the first romantic move, starting with smiles and gazes (of two to three seconds; people have studied this!) and progressing to touching, asking questions, and laughing at jokes. Women are the ones to do this presumably because they are taught to pay close attention to men's body language and to read signals and because they generally do not have the luxury of being totally oblivious. Only after a woman does all of these things does a guy feel like he is "making the first move" by kissing her. This is why it infuriates me when I have to be the brave one to initiate a kiss, after spending the entire night paying such close attention to touches I have given and received that I could recite them, in order, the next day. (Which I do, to my friends.) It would be nice to have some help in doing all of the work necessary to keep our species going.

Missed Connections

A great tragedy: You find a normal, kind-seeming stranger in the wild, a person who presumably hasn't already dated all of your friends. You flirt and it goes well. But you fail to exchange contact information, so they disappear forever as soon as they are out of your eye line. Bonjour, mon frère, you've got a missed connection.

This happens to some degree constantly: most people trying to move pleasantly throughout the world are always low-key flirting, trying to be the polite and sparkly version of themselves. It's easy to think you've had a missed connection with someone who's just acting normal. For example, I once went three days without talking to anyone (I was hiking) and then basically fell in love with the female park ranger at the Rocky Mountain National Park Alpine Visitor Center. She was great! But having gone without human contact for so long, at that point I would have had chemistry with a sentient log.

It's very important to be sure—and this is a warning more for men—that you don't take advantage of another person's politeness. There's no reason you shouldn't talk to a stranger, but people are just going about their lives and don't deserve to be harassed solely because they're on a subway. Allie Jones, writing for *Gawker* (RIP), came up with a guideline: You get two questions. If the other person doesn't engage with you and ask you a question after that, you need to leave them the helk ("hell" + "heck," thank you very much) alone.

I've had only one real missed connection. It was the summer of 2010, days before I got a disastrous set of bangs which would have made the whole thing impossible. (I had asked stylists for years to give me bangs and they had all said no; it turns out they were right.) It was in Chicago; I had just gotten on the red line at the Belmont station, which I mention because it makes me sound legit even though I have only ever lived in Chicago for five months of my life. I was sitting reading *The Girl with the Dragon Tattoo* (remember, it was 2010) when all of a sudden another copy of *The Girl with the Dragon Tattoo* was in my face. Luckily, when I looked up I saw this book was attached to a Hot Dude. He sat down and we started talking about the book, and then about the suburbs where we grew up, about how I was in college and he was in law school, about literature generally and about improv. (This is back when I talked about improv and literature generally, instead of now, when I talk exclusively about the time I killed a fly near my bed and a bunch of tiny maggots exploded out.) I was so enjoying the conversation that I didn't realize we were at my stop until the doors were about to close. I had to jump over Hot Dude and literally run off the train without getting his name. I was a fairy-tale princess disappearing into the night, except instead of an evening dress I was wearing ripped-up salmon-colored pants that, at the time, were my entire personality.

What makes this an actual missed connection? Viewed clinically, this was just a Pleasant Conversation with Someone I Found Hot, made more meaningful by the fact that (a) I am an introvert who usually does not talk to strangers and (b) we live in a world where, as a means to stay alive, I have to assume that most men would like to murder me. But if you're feeling it, it's a missed connection! You don't have to both consider it a missed connection: if you consider it one, it counts. All it really means to call something a "missed connection" is that it would have been a good opportunity to ask for their contact information. Doesn't mean they would have given it to you!

Then again, my roommate Zach (who wants to be credited as "Zach Zimmerman, eligible gay bachelor with a sharp wit and a heart of gold") thinks there's something special to the fact that you *can't* contact this missed connection. Instead, they always live in your mind as this fetal stem cell of a relationship that could have become anything.

In fact, when people *do* try to track down their missed connections I think it's often very creepy, if not very, *very* creepy. Justin

Bieber has *more than once* posted photos of attractive young women on Instagram with captions seeming to implore his followers to figure out who she is so that he can contact her. (I mean, his exact words were "OMG who is this!" but the message comes across.) People on the internet love to track stuff down because it makes them feel like competent TV detectives and because it distracts them from tasks like filing their taxes or going around the table with their families sharing one bad thing and one good thing that happened that day.

But this Justin Bieber–style stalking is not cute. It is very bad! It is doxxing. I am a professional researcher, so maybe I am slightly better at tracking down people's information online, but you can figure out *a lot* about people *very quickly* if you know what words to google (or, better yet, Nexis). It's one thing if you're one professional tracking down a celebrity's information; it's quite another if you're a huge number of people trying to identify and contact a private citizen. Even if you don't have an Instagram following as big as Justin Bieber's, don't do this. People are entitled to their privacy—being hot in public does not waive this right.

3

DATING

Defining the Date

"Was it a date?": the question of our generation. Not in importance, obviously—that's "How do we dismantle white-supremacist capitalist patriarchal power structures?" and "Are we already 100 percent screwed with regard to global warming?" and "Is Amelia Earhart still alive out there?" But "Was it a date?" is our question in terms of being genuinely more difficult to answer now than at previous points in history.

My claim to fame for many years was that, while my entire personality is "on a date," I had never been on one. To some people this sounds disingenuous. My coworker Harris Mayersohn is currently waging a PR war on my propensity to make this type of "I've never" declaration: I told him I'd never dry-humped (which I still maintain I haven't, *as an end in itself*) and that I'd never heard a single song by Diplo (I forgot about "Paper Planes." And "Too Close." And "Elastic Heart." And now that I google it, I realize every song ever made is a Diplo song). And I do have to admit, I'm no longer so sure that I've *never* been on a date.

The platonic ideal of a date, I guess, is an activity you go on with a potential romantic partner, where you agree to spend the evening deciding if you like each other's personalities enough to lick mouths at the end of the night. But that kind of predetermined date is increasingly rare in our more loosely structured dating culture; I have certainly never been on one. One thing we do have is "dates" with people we're already sleeping with. I've spent evenings with guys I'm hooking up with where we go see a friend's poetry night/drag show/a cappella concert before going back to my apartment to respectfully hold hands. But what is gained by classifying that kind of evening as a "date"? I already knew that person was into me! Who cares!

And of course there are the kind of "dates" that end in first kisses, but it's not always clear going in that these are dates. First kisses are always between 50 and 100 percent shocking to me, because before you smooch it's so difficult to tell if the evening is engineered toward kissing. I've gotten close to the platonic ideal of a date, like four-fifths of the way there. But that *almost*-explicitly-a-date date I'm thinking of involved getting drinks twice without even kissing and then hanging out a third time and skipping straight to sleeping together. So who knows! Was only the third one a date? Were they all? Are you and I, reader, on a date *right now*?!

"How can you possibly be so unsure about this?" you incredulously ask. It's possible because we're living through an age when (a) casual sex is normal and (b) smartphones exist. People are either meeting on apps, which helpfully establish the context of "it's a date" for you, or sliding sideways into low-commitment things with friends they've already hung out alone with on a nonsexual basis. I'm not on apps, so I'm stuck with the "Oh wow, I'm all of a sudden alone at a bar at two A.M. with my friend" slide, bypassing the concept of a date altogether. And what's crazy about those slid-into-date-ish-after-all nights is that they were *identical* to previous 100 percent *platonic* evenings with *the exact same dudes.*

It is entirely possible to meet someone organically and say, "Let's go on a date," but I haven't. I *did* once, feeling very proud of myself, say, "Let's get drinks," which is in my opinion synonymous. This went very well until my date mentioned his girlfriend. (More on this in a later chapter because obviously I have *a lot* of thoughts.) It's also entirely possible to realize you have sexual feelings for a friend and say to them, "Let's go on a date," but I am highly skeptical that there has ever been a single person in the world emotionally together enough to do that.

So . . . have I ever really been on a "date"? Well, how much am I supposed to weigh the end of the evening? Does kissing mean it definitely *was* a date the whole time, even if I just thought I was doing a public service by forcing someone to watch *When Harry Met Sally* . . . ? Does *not* kissing mean it definitely wasn't a date? Does my emotional experience count—that it *felt* like a date, even if I botched the landing? If he mentioned "another time I was on a date," does that mean he's referring to *this* as a date?! Okay, then why am I *still alone*?! And conversely: remember that "we went on three maybe-dates but we didn't even kiss on the first two" that I mentioned? At the time, I *agonized* about whether those were dates.

Recently, the dude told me they were definitely dates: Does it matter that I really didn't know if they were at the time?

In fact, that guy referred to that collection of dates—we went on only two more after that before he broke up with me—as "dating." And I was like: [extremely Jerry Seinfeld voice] don't even get me *started* on the word "dating." When people use it to talk about someone they've known for two weeks, I have an aneurysm. (Honestly congrats to me for surviving dozens of aneurysms.) It should be illegal to use the word "dating" if you've been kissing someone for less than six months. It takes at least six months to even know if you've been going on "dates"!

Further complicating all this is the fact that the word "date" has become so fraught, the blank white wall onto which we project so many of our anxieties. "Date" means so many different things to people that it's essentially a meaningless word—kind of like "love," actually! (Love, actually . . . a good title if this book ever gets adapted into a movie. . . .) Ideally I'd toss out the word "date" and make up new, smaller words for each discrete experience. But who am I, Shakespeare?! Also, new, made-up words bug me with such a burning intensity that I have to assume either (a) everyone found Shakespeare extremely annoying in his own time or (b) all those words were already being used but no one wrote them down because they were illiterate or busy *not* abandoning their wife and children. The idea of a "date" is a social construct that's constantly changing to the point that by the time you know what it means, today's teens have already decided it means something entirely different. And according to Moira Weigel in *Labor of Love*, Americans didn't even date until 1900! As long as dating has existed, it has been rapidly evolving in a way that significantly worries old people (anyone who isn't a teen).

Ultimately I think classifying something as a date is basically impossible to the point of being worthless. Better to just communicate how you are feeling to a person and listen to how they are feeling about you. I don't think we could find our way to one unified definition of a "date" at this point. How could we? Maybe we just give one person the power to define it, but who could possibly be wise enough? Oprah? She's busy! She's acting again!

There's maybe a bit of self-indulgence in laboring over whether something was a date, instead of just mustering up the courage to ask. It's dramatic! You get to luxuriate in the drama, the thrill of a budding relationship where you're constantly analyzing clues and significant hangouts. It makes you feel like you're part of a story and therefore the Protagonist. I've begun to realize that wondering whether something was a date is like unrequited love: actually pretty easily resolved, and boring to me. So: Have I ever been on a date? Sure. Tons!

Ways to Make It Clear It's a Date

- ◆ Say, "Thank you for meeting me here for our date."
- ◆ When you finalize plans via text, say, "It's a romantic date!"
- ◆ Fifteen minutes in, say, "What a fun date we are already having!"

- ◆ Mention that in comparison to other *dates* you have been on, this one is better/longer/the most you have ever been asked to discuss the career choices of Nic Cage.
- ◆ Say, "Oh good, this small candle is very romantic, appropriate for our date."
- ◆ Ask the bartender for one Miller High Life for yourself and one for your date.
- ◆ Refer to your socks as your "date socks."

Apps

I am anti-app, though I know I would be going on a lot more dates if I weren't. The whole point of dating apps—the shining dream of a life-hacked future—is to introduce you to every person you could possibly be interested in going on a date with and to provide a context in which you have explicit permission to ask them out. It's like a prince in a fairy tale throwing a mandatory ball for every eligible maiden in the land, except every eligible dude is there, too, and no one has to already know all the moves to a bunch of elaborate group dances. The biggest advantage of apps is, in my mind, that they establish in advance that you are, in fact, *on a date*. (Or meeting up to have casual sex—decide for yourselves, cool kids, if that's a date. I say, Sure, treat yourself, call it a date, you deserve it.)

Unfortunately, there do exist sociopaths who seek to find friends on apps (???), even though these apps exist FOR DATING, hence, "dating apps." I know some apps claim to also be for finding friends, but they're only saying that so they look less pervy. While I totally respect anyone's desire to connect with other humans on a nonsexual level, I firmly believe Hinge is not the place to do that. Being on a dating app to find friends feels to me like a bouncy ball hanging out in the apple display at the grocery store. Like, okay, you seem fun, but I'm here because I'm looking for a very specific thing. If you want friends so bad, go take an improv class.

And while apps allow you to drastically increase the number of first dates you go on . . . I don't want to go on a ton of first dates. I'm busy ALL the time. It's hard enough for me to plan dates with men I'm already sleeping with. It's hard enough to ever see my friends! I rarely get to spend a night alone having fun—and whenever I do any of these things, I'm racked with guilt over not being home, working. The thought of going on dozens of first dates legitimately gives me stress pain in my teeth. Maybe one in 150 guys (if that!) will be both attracted to me and attractive to me. I'm trying to work smart, not hard, and 150 dates seems very hard.

Apps also ask you to commodify yourself in a way that makes me metaphorically nauseous and also kind of physically nauseous. Dating in general can be seen as a competition with everyone else on the planet, but apps ask you to specifically market yourself for a romantic consumer. What photos SELL you as a desirable partner? What bio is your advertising slogan? What six things can't you live without, in a sexy way? I once was on OkCupid and listed 1. ghosts 2. ghosts 3. ghosts 4. ghosts 5. ghosts 6. *National Treasure*. And the consumers HATED it! The whole concept of capitalism, that goods and capital are finite and we are all in competition for them, is a scare tactic to keep us oppressing each other while a select few benefit. The select few in this dating-as-capitalism scenario are, I guess, Leonardo DiCaprio, who is NOT HOT and who dates exclusively blond twenty-year-olds. (Leonardo DiCaprio should, in my opinion, be in jail.)

Even more than I hate commodifying myself, I hate men judging me as a commodity. For thousands of years, women have been throughout their lives reduced to their worth as sexual objects (slash domestic workers). We learn very early on to go to great lengths to increase our sexual value in the eyes of men, without even realizing that's why we're (for example) agonizing over whether our one snack for the day should be a pear or a seventy-calorie sugar-free yogurt. For years—much of my childhood and early twenties—I spent the largest portion of my conscious thought on food and how much I hated and was terrified of my body. It has taken a lot of work to divorce my view of my body and my feelings of romantic worthiness from outside sources. I'm afraid apps would undermine that effort. It just doesn't seem worth it to go on a first date with a guy named Grayson who works in venture capital.

One of the supposed benefits of apps is the choice: there are all these people, thousands and thousands of them, who you would never in a million years meet organically. But there's such a thing as too much choice. I'm not saying that in a koan-esque, go chew on *that* idea kind of way. Like, there are scientific studies that show too much choice makes you less happy. In 1995, Columbia professor Sheena Iyengar did a study that found people were more likely to buy jam when presented with six options instead of twenty-four. (And just like jam, men can be very sweet and are basically pointless on their own.) Other studies have shown that people are more likely to feel disappointed with their decision when given more choices, because it's less likely they made the BEST possible choice. So on apps, we swipe and swipe, always sure there is an even better partner out there.

In reality, I think we are compatible with many different people. Instead of swiping endlessly while watching *Adventure Time*, better to pick someone and try to make it work while watching *Adventure Time*. Is there One Perfect Partner for me out there somewhere? I don't think so? And honestly I would be scared to meet this Ideally Suited for Blythe Person. It sounds like an episode of *Black Mirror*. And maybe it already is; I stopped watching after the Domhnall Gleeson episode. I had gotten what I needed.

Not that I don't understand the desire to find the perfect person! And I'm not saying, "Eh, just settle!" I date people casually but find the idea of commitment difficult, because I imagine marrying this person and watching our small differences turn into huge, bitter problems that ultimately lead to us messily divorcing. My parents are divorced! Divorce seems like the logical conclusion of every relationship to me. But no lovers are without differences, and just as I don't have to date every person I kiss, I don't have to marry every person I date, and I don't have to get or stay married, ever! As my mom once reminded me when I was stressing about potentially quitting my job: "No one stays in one job their entire life. Heck, it'd be weird if you stayed married to one *person* your entire life!"

I like meeting men in the random ways my life throws them at me, even if that means I never get to meet Grayson the venture capitalist. I meet these random men while I'm doing things I already like, so I don't spend our first conversation annoyed about whether I'm wasting my time. And I often meet people because we like the same things and the same people; we're—at least in those areas—compatible. And sometimes it takes me a while to know that I'm interested in someone! Everyone's more or less hot to me, so I almost never feel a burning need to rip any individual dude's clothes off. I once knew a guy for over a year before I saw him competently grill vegetables and was like . . . huh, I guess I want to see you naked.

Good Analog Places to Meet Men

Jury duty. Once every handful of years, you are legally forced to hang out with people who you don't work with and who have never dated any of your friends. It's the perfect time to meet a boyfriend. Date another juror! Date a bailiff! Heck, date a lawyer, although I'm pretty sure that's an automatic mistrial!

The house of a friend you're staying with on vacation. I never would have thought myself capable of having a vacation fling with a tall (Australian!) human rights lawyer, but anything is possible when they literally live in the building where you are crashing with a friend. Sure, I'm hot and a good hang, but the real clincher was the siren song of "immediate proximity at two in the morning." It was almost like being in college, if any men had wanted to kiss me in college!

Art museum. Find a David Hockney. Look for a thin dude with greasy hair. Say something about paint. That's a flirt!

Classes. For . . . I don't know . . . ceramics?

Artist collectives. Join one, or visit one your friend is already a part of. Wander around the shared space until you spot someone hot. Ask him about the parrot he's painting on an old treasure chest.

Cafés. Don't annoy people who are working, obviously. But people who are reading . . . it's like, why are you reading in a *café*? Try gently flirting with those people about Flannery O'Connor. (But remember the two questions rule, *men*!)

Concerts. Until recently I would have said this is not an ideal man-meeting environment. Then I went to an Angel Olsen concert where I was standing next to an attractive dude. While waiting for the show to start, I conscientiously ignored him and instead sent five hundred Snapchats each to people I haven't talked to in years. But when a girl standing in front of me sent her boyfriend to get drinks, she started talking to the attractive guy, a total stranger to her. It's just that easy! The attractive guy said he was in law school, which is exciting to me not because of the money he might one day make but because he can explain to me what is accurate and what is inaccurate about the USA Network legal dramedy *Suits*.

Church?! It could definitely be worth going to church, depending on the guy? I think there's an entire Christian Mingle–sponsored rom-com about this exact thing?

Artistic events put on by your friends. You'll run into people you know, they'll run into people they know, they'll introduce you. And you'll immediately have something to talk to that person about! Also, you'll get to support your friends.

The Brooklyn Borough Hall building. There are a *lot* of twentysomething skateboarders there. I was too intimidated to talk to them, but perhaps you'll have better luck.

Date the Person You Want to Be in the World

Ideally, in any partnership, your partner is a person you admire who inspires you to be a better person. I remember the first time I started kissing a guy who was kind, generous, and always decent to me. "Hmm," I thought, "maybe I will endeavor to be less of a cunt to everyone I meet." It was truly revelatory! But the concept of dating the person you want to be in the world is different than admiring and emulating your partner's traits. It's when you date (or want to date) a person who you, in a significant way, want to *be*. It's a big part of why I lusted for Ezra Koenig before I really knew how to use Twitter. It's probably a big part of why Hillary married Bill Clinton! Or, actually, vice versa!

Part of the female impulse to want to BE the male lover comes from the long and stupid history of young women being forbidden from doing anything other than (a) sitting alone in a room, not talking or (b) cleaning while not talking. Women are socialized to admire and not participate in a way that is so widespread and normalized that it never struck me until I read Claire Vaye Watkins write about "watching boys do stuff" in her life-alteringly good essay "On Pandering." Watkins writes about how, for the first chunk of her life, she spent most of her time not actually doing stuff but just watching boys do stuff. "I've watched boys play the drums, guitar, sing, watched them play football, baseball, soccer, pool, Dungeons and Dragons and Magic: The Gathering." I once tried to explain to a man this phenomenon that Watkins and I and (I would guess) many other women had experienced, but the guy said he didn't quite buy it. Immediately after he said that, I and several women I work with watched this guy and several men we work with try to flip water bottles so they landed neatly on a desk.

Sometimes this men-as-active/women-as-passive dichotomy is acknowledged: in *Clueless*, when Tai tells Travis the skater that she wishes she could bravely jump into a crowd like he did, he says she shouldn't, "'cause if girls did it, what would guys do to impress them?" But this "We're just doing all this to impress you, it's not actually fun" line is like when men used to say, "No, no, women are too *good*, too *pure* to be sullied by having any real say or responsibilities in how the world is run!" It's meant to make you *think* you're somehow the one having all the fun, so that the guys can monopolize all the crowd-surfing.

It was only decades ago that women were socialized to watch instead of do, and many career paths weren't even open to them. Life threw responsibilities at young women faster and more densely than it did young men, so while teen boys across the universe could start bands in the sixties, teen girls had to channel that creative energy into shrieking and wanting to boink Paul McCartney. (Two totally enjoyable things, for sure, but less enjoyable on a sociological level if you don't have the choice of being the one lusted after and shrieked over.) Women have been channeling creativity into romance and taught by society to crush on these Eligible Bachelors for so long that it's very easy to confuse artistic and career admiration for romantic admiration. Like Nora Ephron writes in *I Remember Nothing*: "I can't remember which came first—wanting to be a journalist or wanting to date a journalist."

To men's credit, I *have* seen (kind, sensitive, liberal) men date the people they want to be in the world. But I don't see it as much, and it sometimes seems like men dating creative, together women tend to drain the coolness and life force from them. Probably a lot of the reason why dating the person you want to be in the world is so gendered is because of the whole thing of Professionally Insecure Woke Boys (more on this . . . later) being afraid of dating more successful women and of living in a society that trains men to punish successful women by withholding love. So women have to choose! I choose to (try to) be successful and be punished for it by the men of my era. I live in the hope that in the future a gender-neutral archaeologist will dig up my tweets and say: these deserved more play.

A less gender-specific motivation for dating the person you want to be comes from being, like I am, a porous blob who is very affected by and takes on qualities of her environment, like a tofu marinating in a sauce of hot guys with cool aesthetics. E. Alex Jung wrote about this element of *Call Me by Your Name*, the gorgeous movie starring my young crush Timothée Chalamet, who I hope and believe will one day date me because he wants to be me. Jung identifies "a desire to blur boundaries between the self and the other." Writing about gay male relationships specifically, he says, "His desire is rooted in both the fact that he wants to *be* him as much as he wants to be *with* him." It's thrilling to find someone whose mind and aesthetic and way of dancing and general *vibe* you want to emulate! That's got to be a solid 80 percent of what draws you to people, be they friends or potential boyfriends. And since sadly nobody cool seems to offer How to Be as Hot and Interesting as Me 101 classes, the next best thing is to date someone and hope you absorb some of them by osmosis. If you can get HPV from someone, surely you should be able to get a little bit of their able-to-pick-up-languages-extremely-quickly as well!

It may seem that dating the person you want to be in the world is an unhealthy impulse. However, I don't think it inherently is! Maybe it's the twenty-seven years of absolutely never going to therapy talking, a fact that I am ashamed of and would love to rectify if I weren't so bad at scheduling and unable to wake up earlier to fit an extra hour of activities into my life. But: why *not* be inspired by your partner, I say, screaming in the woods, alone! I believe there is a lot of joy in that. The important distinction here is that you have the freedom to actually execute the achievements and fashion choices and whatever your heart desires that you find inspiring in your partner. And as long as you're not going overboard and trying to exactly copy their look and personality, which Harry Styles is currently doing to ME, but which I find adorable and approve of, then God bless. Of course, maybe I'm wrong about this. Maybe I need to take a hint from the woman I recently saw at Starbucks reading a book titled, simply, *Boundaries*.

If you are going to pull this shit, ideally the influence in the relationship is open and reciprocal. You're Joni Mitchell, and part of James Taylor (or maybe Leonard Cohen?) pours out into your album *Blue* from time to time. And James is writing you "You Can Close Your Eyes" while you're sleeping in the backseat during a road trip, and when you wake up he gives you the song to perform and you're like, "Actually, you can keep it." And it's *cute* when you do it, and not rude at all!

But like—maybe it's not reciprocal. As Hamlet said, there's the flippin' rub, my dude! The hard truth about dating the person you want to be in the world, the hard truth of this whole book, is that I am a woman who is attracted to men in a crazy, VR simulated world that has been running for thousands of years on an algorithm designed to give men enormous legal and cultural power over women. I'm interested in being inspired by my lovers, but if I'm not careful about it, the structural imbalance between us could easily let me slip into watching them do their thing as I neglect mine. And I don't wanna! Watching men do their thing could easily cost me an hour a week that I could be spending finally going to therapy.

Either way, I experience this urge to date my idols less and less. Maybe it's because I just have a more solid sense of my identity and aesthetic, both of which I have stolen from my cool friend Emmy. But lately, though I do *kiss* mostly comedy boys (they're the only people I meet!), I don't try to emulate them. I've started doing a new thing where I crush on people whose lives I would never, ever want. The hope is no longer to copy someone else's self but to enrich my own by learning about shit that I don't already think about constantly (mostly old episodes of *Friends*). And it's nice to admire someone in a way that is zero percent mercenary: there's nothing I'm trying to learn from them that will help me in any way other than becoming a gentler and more loving human. I'm no longer trying to date the person I want to be in the world. I'm trying to be that person.

Performative Chillness

There exists a platonic, true chillness where you genuinely don't spend all your time obsessing over relationships. I used to assume that this came from living a rich and fulfilling life and that I would achieve it only as a fifty-five-year-old woman who runs two different sitcoms, donates most of her billions to charity, and spends her odd free moments thinking about learning how to bake. I now know that true chillness can also come from being so demoralized by American politics that you cannot care about men.

There's also "being chill," wherein through a gargantuan effort you outwardly appear chill even though inwardly you are just roiling. You're going on solo trips to Colorado like some cool-ass chick searching for enlightenment, but the entire time you're hiking to pristine mountain lakes you are exclusively thinking about a guy you kissed twice like eight months ago.

Finally, there is performative chillness. This is where you very pointedly "act chill" in a way that makes it clear to the person who you are dating (or even just, unbeknownst to them, crushing on) that you are pissed or sad.

Barthes gives the example of weeping over some slight or offense and then putting sunglasses on around your lover to "hide" that you've been crying, even though it obviously shows that Something Is Going On since (a) no one wears sunglasses inside and (b) it takes me like fifteen to twenty minutes to find my sunglasses any time I even remember that they exist before I'm leaving the house. It's passive aggression, in a situation where we are now all meant to be passive in an easygoing, emotions-aren't-real way.

The point of this kind of thing, I guess, is to at once have the moral high ground, because you are meeting society's standards of Chill Dating Partner, and ALSO punish your lover/hook-up partner/husband/crush by making them figure out clues. You're telegraphing, "Hello, you did something I am not happy about and it is so freaking obvious if you could take a g. d. moment to think about it."

My version of performative chillness is to act very amenable and nonplussed in person and then when I am alone I furiously subtweet the situation. I'm also a fan of unfriending/unfollowing/ deleting phone numbers and lying on my bed looking at a stain on the ceiling until he notices or texts me and I can reply, "I am so sorry but I don't have your number saved—who is this? [baby angel emoji]"

Hopefully your partner takes the hint and solves the puzzle of why you are so obviously misperforming chillness and then addresses the problem. But even if they don't, you get the pleasure of feeling really mad that this person is absolutely RUINING YOUR LIFE and NOT EVEN READING YOUR TWITTER!!! Eventually you have to decide if you want to bring all of this up and try to discuss the problem in case he has no idea that any of this is even happening, OR if you want to just cut him out of your life and never explain why.

One of the big flaws with this system is that in my experience men generally do not want to investigate subtle emotional meltdowns. Whereas when people I care about are acting pissed I try to assess the information and figure out what's wrong like an emotional Nancy Drew, I find that when you show any sort of negative feelings to guys they often just, like, ignore it until it goes away. This makes me believe that the Hardy Boys must be a series of books about two brothers (cousins?) who discover a mystery and spend the next 175 pages walking in the opposite direction.

Ways to Kill Time While You're Waiting to Answer a Text

Nominally, these tips are for distracting yourself while you wait to respond to a text just long enough to seem "cool," "chill," "busy," like a person "whose life consists of things other than texting." In actuality I use most of these while waiting to RECEIVE texts, although in those cases it hypothetically should be easier to kill time because there's nothing I can do about it and I am really just continuing to exist.

Shower. There was a period in my life where basically the ONLY time I didn't have greasy hair was when I was waiting for a guy to text me back. I am proud to say I now wash my hair for other reasons. However I still do not and will never BRUSH it.

Be in Peru and Have No Wi-Fi. I went to Peru immediately after meeting a new guy and it for SURE extended our flirtation by three months, because I took approximately eight hours to respond to any of his texts. Hot!

Sit in a Chair Next to Your Phone and Do Nothing.
Sure, it is very hard and seemingly very pointless to just sit next to your phone, NOT using it to respond to a text. But haven't you heard about that psychology experiment where kids wait to eat marshmallows and are rewarded for their patience with more marshmallows? They proved that the kids who waited weren't any more successful in life, but you get to feel like you accomplished something, I guess.

Think About a Riddle. Once, while avoiding READING a text that I was pretty sure was a dude rejecting me, I thought about a riddle he told me. It bought me about twenty solid minutes before I caved, had a FRIEND read the text, learned I had in fact been rejected, and immediately left the party I had just gotten to. And guess what! I never solved the riddle!

Watch *The Americans.* It's a standout of the "but REALLY it's about marriage!" genre.

Read Up on the Cotard Delusion. Also called "walking corpse syndrome," this is a rare mental illness in which one believes that they are already dead. This is how I feel when multiple people haven't texted me back.

Call Your Senators. If your senators are doing fine, call your representatives. Call your governor! Hell, call your city council member. They might actually pick up.

Being Chill

Being chill: acting like you don't care. Regulating your emotions and doling them out in small doses, so as not to kill anyone, like Cary Elwes does to himself with poison in *The Princess Bride*. This, apparently, is how we are now supposed to conduct ourselves while dating.

Much like not thinking about a polar bear, trying to be chill is impossible. That impossibility makes you more obsessed, to the point that you feel as if every second of your life is spent resisting the urge to text someone. You're doing constant calculations of exactly how much of what you're feeling is "chill" to show. Because you don't want to seem *completely* uninterested! You don't want to end up like Jane Bennett in *Pride and Prejudice*, so careful to appear proper in her courtship with Mr. Bingley that he is easily convinced she doesn't care about him at all. On the other hand: Does that kind of thing ever actually happen? Isn't the most attractive thing in the twenty-first century to act like you don't give a shit at all, like you're just some sort of rock? Rocks are sexy, right?

Showing our emotions, we're convinced, would make us look needy. As *The Rules* writes, "play hard to get!" (Or at least *The Rules* as I understand them from reading the Wikipedia page and watching that episode of *Sex and the City* where Charlotte tries to convert to Judaism.) So you wait to text. You say you're busy on nights you're not busy. You don't get offended when they do these same things to you. You don't ask them for much, you don't rely on them for emotional support. You never mention that you've discussed them with your friends, and you carefully avoid any language that makes it seem as if you believe yourselves to be in any kind of relationship. When you encounter them in the outside world you curl into a ball and roll away like an armadillo. As Alana Massey writes in her essay "Against Chill," "It is a game of chicken where the first person to confess their frustration or confusion loses." And, of course, you're spending a huge, unchill amount of time *thinking* about how to be chill.

And then, because of this immense pressure not to care, anything they do that *isn't* chill becomes, seemingly, hugely significant. I've thought that men were in love with me because we were on the same page about texting frequency. In actuality this is indicative of nothing. I know that my male best friend Todd loves me, even though he is horrible at texting. Texting him feels like writing my questions onto a piece of paper and throwing them into a bottomless cavern. Seen through that lens, it's very impressive that I get a response around 20 percent of the time!

It is very dumb that we are all trying so hard to act like we don't care about the people we're kissing. Playing hard to get has never worked for me—not even close. Conversely, when a guy I like is playing hard to get—being unresponsive to texts or difficult to schedule a date with—it doesn't make me like him more, it just annoys me. And while some people might have self-esteem issues that make it hard for them to accept romantic interest, you shouldn't make that the foundation of your dating strategy.

Charlotte Lieberman, writing in *Cosmopolitan* about the phenomenon of being chill, cites *Guyland* author Dr. Michael Kimmel and sociology professor Dr. Lisa Wade to argue that in acting chill, women are essentially taking on the traditionally "masculine" behavior of not expressing emotions and avoiding vulnerability. This is something men are socialized to do from a young age, taught that true men are stoic. It honestly sucks that dudes are taught to do this, and women doing the same thing is a classic pitfall of (white) feminism: instead of inventing our own power structures and abolishing gender roles in a way that promotes true equality and compassion, we just coopt failed masculine structures and roles. Instead of encouraging *everyone* to be honest and open while pursuing love, we just pointedly wait forty-five minutes before texting back.

Todd (he of sucks-at-texting fame) once told me, after three months of helping me figure out if a guy was into me, that attraction isn't binary; it's on a spectrum. I gasped. I asked him to repeat that idea to our other female roommate. She gasped. It changed my life! Not right away—it takes me, like, three years to learn any lesson (wear gloves when it's cold outside!)—but it did. And I realized that if I am anywhere on the spectrum of being interested in someone, I only like them MORE if I know they are into me. It's nice to know I won't be rejected! It's nice not to have to roll out the "Blythe Is Hot and Interesting" PowerPoint to convince them to go on a date! So let people know you like them. We only live once, and briefly. Whether or not people are into you, being your un-chill self speeds up the process.

The Rules Versus My Rules If I Wrote a Dating How-To Book

1. **Be a "Creature Unlike Any Other"** versus I Am Boring and Like to Stay Inside Watching *Queer Eye*
2. **Don't Stare at Men or Talk Too Much** versus Make Men Listen to You Do Elaborate Bits
3. **Don't Talk to a Man First (and Don't Ask Him to Dance)** versus Walk Up to Men at Parties and Say, "So What's Your Deal?"
4. **Don't Call Him and Rarely Return His Calls** versus Text Him Three Times in a Row, Find a Picture of a Naked Raccoon You Really Want to Text Him, Agonize Over It—but Eventually End Up Texting Him Four Times in a Row
5. **Always End Phone Calls First** versus Any Person Under Forty Who Calls Another Person Is a Murderer
6. **Don't Accept a Saturday Night Date After Wednesday** versus Tell Them You Can't Go on a

Date Because You Have to Stay in and Write,
Then Thirty Minutes Later Text Back, "Ugh
Whatever I'll Be Bad."

7. **Don't Meet Him Halfway or Go Dutch on a Date**
versus Pay More Than Your Fair Share and Say,
"I'm a Sagittarius, the Most Generous Sign in the
Zodiac."

8. **Always End the Date First** versus When They
Say, "I'm Going Home Now," Slump Over and
Say, "Noooo . . . This Is So Sad . . ."

9. **No More Than Casual Kissing on the First Date**
versus Honestly Congrats for Knowing You're
on a Date, Do Whatever You Want During and
Afterward

10. **Don't Rush into Sex and Other Rules for
Intimacy** versus Have Sex Exactly as Early or
Late as You Want! Once I Wanted to Kiss a Guy
but Not Sleep with Him, So I Asked Him to
Leave My Apartment and We Made Out for
Thirty Minutes on a Bench Outside My Door!

11. **Stop Dating Him If He Doesn't Buy You a
Romantic Gift for Your Birthday or Valentine's
Day** versus If He Buys You a Romantic Gift on
Valentine's Day Have a Panic Attack and Ask
Every Woman in Your Phone What Is Going On

12. **Don't See Him More Than Once or Twice a
Week** versus Text Him Very Frequently About
How You Wish You Could Hang Out, but You

Have So Many Deadlines That Your Mouth
Psychosomatically Feels Like It's on Fire???

13. **Don't Tell Him What to Do** versus Tell a Man
He's a Misogynist at Least Once per Date

14. **Don't Expect a Man to Change or Try to
Change Him** versus Slowly Indoctrinate Every
Man into Radical Intersectional Feminism

15. **Don't Open Up Too Fast** versus Tell Him You're
Writing a Book Called *How to Date Men When
You Hate Men*

16. **Be Honest but Mysterious** versus Tell Him the
Scientific Reasons Why When You're on Your
Period You Poop More

17. **Love Only Those Who Love You** versus Actually
This One Is Good

Talking To

I never understood when people used to tell me that they had a
person they were "talking to," as if that were something significant. Uhh, yeah, I "talk to" dozens of people a day, most of whom
probably don't even know my name even though we've worked together for over two years. So if you just have some dude you're
"talking to," it would appear that you and I are both single, friendo.
Especially since "talking to" refers not to face-to-face interactions
but rather to talking on your phone, either via text or, I don't know,
whatever the teens are using (Instagram DMs??).

I first heard of "talking to" in the summer of 2012, when I worked at a Victoria's Secret in a mall in the northern suburbs of Chicago. I spent my days measuring people's boobs and making up facts about primer. (They usually had me work in the beauty section, which, if you've ever seen my face, is hilarious.) Working at Victoria's Secret was honestly one of the most feminist experiences of my life and I took studious notes for a novella about it before remembering that I don't know how to write fiction. One of my coworkers was "talking to" a guy who was in the military, so instead of going on dates, they were flirty texting.

(Also: I've met some people recently who use the phrase "talking to" interchangeably with "hooking up." At first I panicked that I was sounding like a virginal moron by assuming that talking might actually mean, you know, talking, but Urban Dictionary lists both meanings. Shakespeare's been dead for ten million years, but the English language just keeps giving, baby!)

Maybe you'd like an example of "talking to" from popular culture? Well, consider "Panda," that song where they keep saying "Panda" over and over. In "Panda," then-teen Desiigner declares that he has broads who live in Atlanta. BUT: he admitted to *Billboard* magazine that he had never been to Atlanta. The broad (yes, just the one) he was referring to was a girl he was solely talking to over Facebook. "We never met in person," Desiigner told *Billboard*. "She just said she was from ATL, so I was like, 'All right—I got broads in Atlanta.'"

Perhaps this sounds very fishy to you, as my bra-shilling coworker's romantic situation did to me! But I am happy to report that one day I sat down and thought very hard about it, like that meme of a brain expanding from plain cheese pizza to pepperoni pizza to pineapple pizza until it's a whole human radiating light, representing a pineapple with pepperoni embedded inside of it. Which is to say: I now believe talking to is real. There is a huge intimacy to texting about nothing for hours a day. You tell stories and discover each other's interests, in turn opening up new things you can randomly text each other about. (Which means, of course, that you braved that first horrible stage where you can only text about your jobs and your mutual friend Jeff at whose birthday drinks you met.) You create inside jokes. You learn how the other person expresses laughter. (You thought their "ha ha" was sarcastic at first, and it almost ruined you!) Honestly: It's a blast. It's a joy!

If you're texting a person all day in the way talking to implies, you're doing a solid amount of thinking up bullshit reasons to text them. That's something I don't do with my female friends unless I'm alone at a concert and the opener just finished and now I have to wait approximately five hours for the main act to start. And when a dude texts that frequently—holy shit. Because in my experience, many men are bad at texting. Probably this is because women are socialized to be expert communicators, the better to perform emotional labor with—Who cares, what matters is that "many men are bad at texting" is extremely true and it is driving me to madness. (Barthes said, "The lover's fatal identity is precisely this: *I am the one who waits*," but I feel that is the phone-owning woman's fatal identity.) So if a male human I barely know texts me, "What should I get my mom for her birthday?" I take that as proof that he is very into me. A great example of dumb nothingness you make up to keep up a talking to relationship is everything in the movie *You've Got*

Mail. All of Meg Ryan's and Tom Hanks's emails are completely insane and pointless—a butterfly on the subway? Uh . . . great? But that's how you know they're falling in love.

So, all things considered, I agree with Desiigner. There was a time I would have considered myself to have a broad in Europe. But now he is ignoring me! HELLO!!!! IF YOU ARE READING THIS BOOK PLEASE RESPOND TO THE DIRECT QUESTION I ASKED YOU OVER TEXT!

I don't really blame him though—most of my talking to's fizzle out. The guys live far away, the timing wasn't right, or we just didn't have the chemistry in person that we did via text. Is that a feature of talking to? Are all relationships born from an extended period of texting doomed to end up fading away quietly or, worse, ending like the one in Kristen Roupenian's short story "Cat Person"? In that story, a young woman meets an older man and gets into a groove of texting him. They come up with inside jokes and make discoveries about each other like "We have both at some point owned cats!" Based on that small amount of information and the much larger assumptions she projects onto him, the young woman agrees to go on what ends up a disastrous date. You may remember that when this story came out, every woman in the entire world was like, "It me! Dating sucks! The world is a cesspool! All heterosexual sex is rape!"

As I wrote earlier, it is definitely very common and normal to project onto a romantic interest you barely know. (If you are a man I have talked to more than once, ask me about the detailed sixty-year future I've imagined for us.) I don't think that this is unique to relationships that are, in their early days, text-heavy. Either way, you eventually learn things about the other that don't fit with the image of them you've imagined. Maybe it just takes slightly longer to discover this via text because it's easier to be on your best behavior when you have five seconds to think about whether you really want to make that bad joke. (My illusions are always shattered by particularly bad jokes.)

I will say that I advocate for knowing the person a little bit in person before getting into a serious text flirtation, so that you're basing your projections on at least a foundation of reality. In the case of someone you've met on a dating app, waiting to text a ton until you've gone on a date ensures that you're not burning first-date topics or wasting precious text charm on someone who turns out to be a dullard! It is truly deranged that Shopgirl and NY152 don't officially "meet" until the final scene of *You've Got Mail*. They get a pass from me because AOL was new then. They didn't know any better. You, reader, do!

To answer the younger and dumber version of myself who didn't believe talking to was real: The internet is real. Your phone is real. What happens on those things happens to you in your real life. I once sent letters back and forth with a guy for a year before we kissed—did I consider that realer? If anything, it was less real, because it was less frequent and more thought out and involved more poems (kill me).

Schrödinger's Relationship

Schrödinger's Cat is a thought experiment that we all have heard of and know enough about to "get" *New Yorker* cartoons about it.

There is a cat in a box, and unless you go and check on it, for some reason it is at once both alive and dead. This relates to quantum mechanics in some way. Cool, fine.

Schrödinger's Relationship is a tactic to ensure you are not *not* dating somebody by avoiding ever "checking" on the status of what's up. This tactic is useful if having your fledgling relationship status be in quantum superposition is more appealing to you than outright NOT dating that person and also is not as scary to you as bringing it up and getting rejected. So basically, this is a strategy if you, like me, are a romantic coward. Or if you, like someone much more sophisticated than I, luxuriate in the vagaries of human existence.

The main way of reaching this state of quantum idiocy is by being very careful during the early stages of a relationship—everything before you kiss, basically—to never refer to anything you are doing as a "date." Of course, everything you're doing could reasonably be called a date: you're getting dinner, you're getting late drinks, you're getting dinner and then going to a museum for fifteen minutes because you didn't realize they were about to close and then getting drinks instead. BUT. Depending on how the person feels about you, they might be thinking of those things as just chill hangs.

By never referring to these activities as "dates," you never give the other person the opportunity to say, "Hold up, whoa whoa whoa, this is NOT a date." Presumably followed by "Ew, gross, I would never go on a date with you. That you thought this was a date proves your entire perception of the world is skewed and is why you will never have a healthy relationship and also why you can't figure out why other people love *Breaking Bad* so much." (Hon-

estly: This guy is rude! You wouldn't want to date him anyway!
Also, *Breaking Bad* is not a good show!)

So instead of referring to these as "dates," you basically just
have to refer to everything as "getting drinks." God forbid you
swing too far on the other side of the spectrum and use language
that makes it seem like you view all this as platonic! In a pinch I
have used "hanging out," but that's borderline. Hanging out is what
I did with my friends growing up when we were bored and too
young to drive and had already put our friend's bike up a tree.
And apparently to today's teens "hanging out" just means casual
sex. All of human language is really failing me in my attempt to
maybe possibly not be *not* dating this dude!

Less of a frequent problem but just as important, you have to
make sure to never define in speech or writing what this person's
relationship is to you. This means being very careful while introducing them to people, and also not texting them anything like "I
told my roommate I couldn't go to their Empowerment Seminar
for Girl Bosses Who Love Leaning In to Capitalism because I was
getting drinks with my friend, Dave." "FRIEND?!" Dave had just
built up the confidence to make a real move, and now he thinks
you are telling him you only want to be friends, which, though he
is disappointed, he is ultimately fine with because he knows that
the "friend zone" is not a thing.

In an ideal world, I know, we would all just be completely honest and speak the truth that is in our heart. But what does that look
like here? You can't be like "This is the guy I've been out with three
times and haven't kissed and I'm starting to get really in my head
about it" or "This is the girl I'm sleeping with out of a mixture of

genuine fondness, geographical convenience, and seasonal affective disorder." Whenever I back myself into a corner where I'm already introducing my Romantic Interest to someone but remember in time not to call them my "friend," I fall back on just not contextualizing them in any way: "This is . . ." [blinks slowly while smiling bigger and bigger until my entire head is my mouth] ". . . Dave." [Nods vigorously because I have prolonged by five minutes the illusion that Dave and I may be dating.] This makes it seem like I suck at introductions, which I emphatically DO NOT! I am very proud of being, like, okay at introductions, and I plan to slowly improve over the next twenty to seven hundred years.

By doing all of this, by continuing to do date-like activities, you will be simultaneously dating and hanging out as just friends. The problem here is that eventually, you do have to check on the cat because, well, you want to kiss the cat, and there's no point waiting five hundred years to do it. Not only is life short, but as Dr. Helen Fisher writes in her book *Anatomy of Love*, "People almost never become captivated by someone they know well." And after a while, if you're hanging out and having fun and not hooking up, you are likely just friends. (Which is not a bad thing! Friends are lovely and important and you can definitely kiss people you're friends with.) But depending on how often you're hanging out, this strategy tops out at maybe a month, before you have to either kiss or get off the pot.

But remember that another tenet of quantum physics is that if an electron has a 50 percent chance of being in place A and 50 percent of being in place B, just because you find the electron in place A does not mean that it is not also—in some alternate dimension—in place B. So even if in this dimension it turns out that you and Dave are not dating, take solace in knowing that mathematically, in one of countless parallel universes, you might be.

This ISN'T a Date!

Because all the men I have ever met have some mix of social anxiety disorder and seasonal affective disorder, and because I seem to primarily attract men who broke up with their long-term girlfriends mere MOMENTS ago, I often find myself hooking up with men who "can't date anyone right now." This is entirely fine with me. I am not trying to trick men who aren't totally aboard the SS *Blythe Is Hot and Fun* into marrying me. I'm not trying to trap men! Except Harry Styles, but I'm not trying to trap him into dating me, I'm just trying to trap him.

Recently I've discovered that I, too, can't date anyone right now. I have a lot of work that I am very behind on, to such a degree that it sometimes makes my hands feel like they are on fire. I also have what are probably unrealistic ideas about what a partner should be and a crippling fear of dealing with the logistics of breaking up with someone. Moving makes me sob anyways; having to move because a man doesn't love me anymore? I'd likely have to return to Antioch, Illinois, to float in a swamp for the rest of my life.

So I appreciate men being honest with me about their emotional availability. I LESS appreciate (in that I absolutely resent) men not trusting me when I say I'm not trying to date them, either. There's a difference between clearly communicating your availability and yelling, "I CAN'T BE IN ANYTHING SERIOUS RIGHT

NOW," every time you cum. Men often position their I-don't-want-to-date-you speeches to me as if they're looking out for me, which they probably mean in a kind way but which comes off as infantilizing. I don't want or need a man looking out for me.

When I'm hooking up with these men who can't be in anything serious, the anxiety of "Is this a date?" flips. I'm not wondering or hoping that it's a date in that way that I'm not sure if they're interested in me sexually—we're already sticking our tongues in each other's ears. They like me. Instead, I'm trying to telegraph that This Is Not a Date. As in: even though we're seeing a play and then going home to discuss the play calmly and thoughtfully (this is what I call sex), I'm not trying to become your girlfriend.

Men—not the men that I'm boning, but third parties whom I have begged for advice enough times that they are now enmeshed in my psychodrama—have argued to me that doing this kind of thing *is* dating, whether I like it or not. "It is SO IRONIC that YOU of ALL PEOPLE don't realize you're DATING!" they shriek, arms flailing. But I believe you can have fun in a hangout capacity with someone you're sleeping with without "dating." Like, why not? Going over to bone someone who lives on the opposite side of the city from you is going to eat up your whole evening anyways, so it just makes sense to have dinner together first. Remember that the word "date" is so divorced from any concrete meaning that you can make it contain or not contain anything you dang well please.

(If not "a date," how do I refer to these evenings? I once went with "thick dick appointment," a phrase gifted to me by my friend and beauty angel Phoebe Robinson. But people hated this. Everyone I said "thick dick appointment" to visibly cringed. One friend who especially hated it asked me to come up with "a chaste euphemism like the rest of us disgusting perverts," so I decided on calling them "knitting circle." My friend immediately forgot and when I told him a couple days later that I was busy with knitting circle, he insisted I invite his new girlfriend, who loved to knit.)

For a long time, I wondered what exactly it was about me that made all men assume I was trying to seriously date them. Did I watch too many Nora Ephron movies while my brain was still squishy, causing me to seep out a rom-com vibe? Or maybe I'm just too good at small talk? Do people think I'm trying to date them because I ask them questions about themselves?

Maybe, yeah. We live in a culture that encourages women to be emotionally perceptive and emotionally open but discourages men from being those things. While women are socialized to be emotionally intimate with friends, men are told they should only be emotionally intimate with romantic partners. (If even then!) So when I just talk about my day and ask a dude questions about his, trying to be supportive in a way that is extremely standard for my female-socialized self, men might easily read all that as SHE IS CARING ABOUT MY EMOTIONS, therefore SHE IS TRYING TO DATE ME. I can understand why they would feel that, considering! It explains why men view their mates as their best friends more often than women do. It also explains why marriage is more rewarding for men; unmarried men are more likely to be lonely and to die alone, sooner, than unmarried women are.

This theory, that men assume I want to date them because they are socialized to confine emotional connection to romantic relationships, feels very true to me. I was proud of myself when I thought of it! I tweeted it! I may have texted one ex! But, in the interest of complete honesty, I am sure that at one time I *did* seem intensely interested in dating. For much of my life I *was* stressed about never having had a boyfriend. I would never *admit* to that stress; like the stress of hating my body, it was both something society encouraged me to constantly feel and something surface-level "girl power" feminism said I should just *stop* feeling. (I don't totally hate Girl Power—I hate to think where we'd be without *Spice World*—but breaking free of gendered oppression is going to take more than cute sayings and blow-up plastic armchairs with cartoon flowers on them.) By now I think I've moved past my "I've never seriously dated, there's something hugely wrong with me!" stress. In fact, I'm low-level stressed that, while I don't want a boyfriend, I might, if I'm not vigilant, accidentally acquire one. BUT I still do want a certain level of flirty repartee, text responsiveness, and acknowledging-me-as-a-human from people I kiss.

There is quite a difference, though, between considering something Not a Date when the other person frantically doesn't want to date you versus when they maybe do. When they do, it feels much worse! When I suspect that someone maybe does want to be boyfriends, letting them make me food and me touching their knee in public feels like leading them on. I worry that I'm draining them of time and care and not offering the security of a label in return, like a succubus but for vegan food and cuddles.

Now that *I* have the guilty conscience, I can respect why dudes have felt compelled to set timers on their phones to remind me every four and a half hours that they can't date me. Being communicative is the mature, healthy thing to do. You just have to avoid sounding patronizing, like they're the earth's biggest morons for thinking you could ever love them—especially when you're not entirely sure that's what they're after.

But it's maybe a bummer to have these what-are-we check-in talks at all. The very act of observing and discussing something changes it. I once saw a (bad) play called *Heisenberg* that had nothing to do with physics but was about two people trying to avoid putting a label on their relationship. It took me a solid eighteen hours to understand the reference, but when I got there I was very impressed.

4

PSYCHIC
WOUNDS

Men Weaponizing the Bechdel Test

The Bechdel Test is a criterion for judging films that was created by cartoonist Alison Bechdel in her comic strip *Dykes to Watch Out For*. It requires that a movie have at least two (named) women who talk to each other about something other than a man. The test is a quick, easy way to judge whether any group of movies (say: everything currently in theaters) is sexist. It's such a simple metric, but it really snaps into view how many mainstream films (around 40 to 50 percent!) either don't feature women or use women only as devices to further stories about men, to provide exposition or eye candy or cheap stakes (i.e., I'm doing this heist to get back my estranged hot wife, who had one line in the whole movie!!!). It's not surprising that in real life men treat women as disposable, as less real, like their desires and preferences and consent matter less than a man's, when films tell men that women are just props and that men are the protagonists.

And yet, there are men who would use this tool for female

representation against me (a woman)! YOU: [gasps.] ME: I KNOW!!!
A story:

I cohost a live comedy show about science with my friend Madelyn. It's called The Scientists (we are not scientists). Starting a show about science was exciting and nerve-racking and required months of prep (remember: I am not a scientist. I read novels for my college degree. One time, in lieu of a final paper, I wrote the first thirty pages of a screenplay about how Kanye West was the early aughts' Great Gatsby. And I probably got, like, a B in that class). Before I perform in any live show I want to puke, but before that first Scientists show, about to get up onstage and assert that Madelyn and I had some authority to joke about artificial intelligence—it felt like my insides were being puréed and then heated on a low setting. But: we got onstage and screamed about robots! It was dope!

The next day, I got a nastygram from some dude with two first names who had apparently been in the audience the night before. The email consisted of paragraph-long numbered criticisms of our show, more specifically our hosting job, and even more specifically, me. This dude needed very badly to tell me that he was offended/disappointed/mad that I had spent time (at most five minutes in an hour-and-a-half show) talking about how (Irish actor) Domhnall Gleeson and (Google engineer) Jeff Dean are Hot to Me. Wrote this dude: "Basically you would barely pass a Bechdel Test **in this real life event.**" (The bold and underlining are his, obviously. Who emphasizes things that way? It looks ugly and I consider it a macroaggression!)

This man had taken the Bechdel Test, a tool created to highlight how little women are allowed to say in culture, and used it to police my language in the show I cohost with another woman. A show **about science**. (See?)

I felt so ashamed after reading this guy's email. I had been incredibly nervous about hosting The Scientists without any real qualifications other than my enthusiasm and my ability to read many articles, over months of preparation. After reading this email I was like, Oh, I am an unserious moron.

Obviously NOW I realize this isn't true, and I realize that email was kind of hilarious and that guy was a real dick for sending it. I never responded, so on the off chance that dude is reading this book (which he isn't; I checked, he doesn't follow me on Twitter), here's what I have to say.

First of all, how DARE you insult Domhnall Gleeson by questioning my right to call him hot.

Secondly, helluhr, we passed the Bechdel Test.

1. Two women (Madelyn, me)
2. Who talk to each other (our banter is the whole point of the show)
3. About something other than a man (yes, in this case about whether robots will decide humans are useless and cut us up into atoms)

There is no fourth requirement that the women *never* mention men, as if they had been beamed into some totally man-free universe, which, if it meant that no know-it-all misogynists could email me at will, I would be interested in visiting! Maybe this dude thought he was signing up for a science show hosted by someone more along the lines of Neil deGrasse Tyson. Maybe email dude thinks science is only serious if it's about how technically BB-8 would have skidded uncontrollably on sand, not about how technically the star of *Ex Machina* is my new boyfriend. It's absolutely any person's right to not enjoy my comedy. It is also absolutely fucked up for a man to try to use the Bechdel Test against me.

It's not inherently unserious for me to talk about crushes. If I treat female emotions and interiority as real, then it is not demeaning to talk about my emotions regarding men. It's expressing my flipping lived human experience. The Bechdel Test is just women asking to be the center of our own stories and to have the opportunity to tell those stories without some rando dude riding our asses about it.

The thing about the idea that talking about love is frivolous is that it is applied only to women. When men do the same thing they are carefully observing the nuances of the human heart, and Pulitzers get thrown at them. Roxane Gay, in her essay collection *Bad Feminist*, points out that stories about the domestic sphere are only considered minor when written by women: "Consider the work of John Updike or Richard Yates. Most of their fiction is grounded in domestic themes that, in the hands of a woman, would render the work 'women's fiction.'"

Ideally, I want to write and think about MANY things over the course of my life, most of which are not Domhnall Gleeson. These include fighting white supremacy, bigotry, and patriarchy; reversing Republican gerrymandering; and overplanning road trips. It would be very dope if I could someday live in a world in which I could practice a feminism that gives, as Chimamanda Ngozi Adichie recommends, less "space to the necessity of men." (May God forgive me from quoting a statement in which Adichie was criticizing Beyoncé.) But at the moment, the two big obstacles to me not talking about men are (1) men are oppressing me and (2) I want to kiss them all.

So I'm not Neil deGrasse Tyson. If I were, *StarTalk* would feature a B-plot every week where two asteroids fall in love. (Please, Neil, @ me.)

Scale of One to Ten

There are some things that were always bad but that gained widespread recognition as such only after Donald Trump endorsed them. Among these are KFC, taco bowls, and ranking women on a scale of one to ten. This was always, always, fucked up, but it used to be, like, a "funny" thing men did in real life and on sitcoms. But now that Trump is president, it's government policy!

Here's what I realized, after a long time of feeling amorphously uncomfortable with ranking women on a scale of one to ten, and to be completely honest, a long time before that being so deep into the patriarchal simulacrum that it didn't seem weird to me and I was very dog-drinking-coffee-while-the-house-burns-down "this is fine": reducing women to a number based solely on how much their physical appearance makes the ranker want to fuck them is extremely dehumanizing. Women have worth based on things other than their appearance. This isn't a one-to-ten ranking scale. This isn't even a two-axis graph. It isn't a three-axis graph, the most complicated thing I learned before shutting my heart and mind to math because [picks up calculus equation] IT DIDN'T SPARK JOY. Ranking women should be illegal or at LEAST as complicated as a twelve-dimensional graph. (Don't even try to imagine this in your head. Just look it up on Google Images.)

And anyways, there is absolutely no use to this ranking system. Different people find different things sexy, so it's not like you're providing a useful metric that can be used by everyone to save time, like a credit score. (Also I feel like credit scores are fake, but that's a topic for my second book, *How to Date Men When Credit Scores Are Fake*.) And what's the difference between a woman who is an eight and a woman who is a ten? Presumably they are both incredibly hot women, but now one of them has been made to feel insecure and like she needs to buy Dove body wash.

The mere idea of people being sorted into "leagues" of hotness is completely divorced from reality. One of the great realizations of adult life is that anybody can fuck anybody. Desire is complicated, and bonkers, and random, and I have kissed some men who are much, much hotter than me. Whatever! Everyone is just horny and trying to be loved.

I'm not quite sure how to deal with men who rank women on a scale of one to ten, beyond my go-to move of pretending that I am Prue on *Charmed* and imagining using telekinesis to stab these men with the sharpest and most phallically shaped object in the room. Some women choose to call themselves a ten, asserting that they are at the top of the scale and there is nothing you can do about it. While I do often refer to myself as hot (because . . . I am hot), when I rank myself on a scale of one to ten I lately refer to myself as a one. I think there is more power in saying I am worth nothing in your system but I will destroy you anyways. While I find this very funny/sexy/strong/powerful, me calling myself a one makes other people very sad and uncomfortable. I think this is because they know that now that Trump is president, I will be denied voting rights for being too ugly (I mean, I'm going to be denied them anyway eventually for being a woman). The only reason I am still allowed to vote at this point is because I am on three acne medications which are CURRENTLY WORKING!

A Better Ranking Scale, for Men I Am Into

Hot, in my opinion: +5

Dressed like a Columbia professor: +2

Actual Columbia professor: +4

Dressed like Jughead on *Riverdale*: +200

Dressed like Jughead on *Riverdale* for Halloween but normally dressed like a Columbia professor: +500

Not trying to make it in comedy: +7

Very funny: +4

Too tall for me to easily kiss: +5

Likes hiking: +5

Has put out an album called *Sweet Baby [Insert Own First Name]*: +6

Motivated about or interested in anything at all: +15

Has lots of good photos online so I can show my
    friends that he is, in fact, hot to me: +5
Good at drawing: +4
Literally just listens to women when they talk: +200

PDA

In middle school, it's hammered into our heads that public displays of affection are gross and a moral blight on society. After dress code violations, it's basically the number one thing teachers scan for in the halls, ready and eager to punish, certainly more than bullying or, like, general overcrowding caused by a breakdown in the American educational system. Teachers constantly lecture us about PDA; even seemingly unrelated lessons on gravity come with the caveat that "saying 'all things with mass gravitate toward one another' is no defense for PDA." There probably would have been a D.A.R.E. for PDA if they could have come up with a good acronym, and it's a shame that there wasn't because those shirts would be an incredibly solid retro/ironic look.

Not that sex positivity means that you should be letting middle schoolers go wild during passing period; they're minors and they do need to get to social studies to learn about Thomas Paine. But it is slightly weird that adults spend so much time thinking and talking about preteens holding hands and casually kissing. Did the teachers think kids were going to start having sex in the hallways if not constantly reminded that it was in direct violation of the student handbook?

I wouldn't know, because when I was in the seventh grade no boys were trying to even hold my hand. The anti-PDA warnings we were given constantly reminded me of this: kissing is an epidemic that is affecting everyone except you, a nerd no one wants to touch.

To this day I am generally anti-PDA. It probably has something to do with all of those warnings, and also something to do with the fact that it's incredibly rude to have sex in the back of a cab! Cab drivers are human beings, what is wrong with you people?! That being said, it's very difficult to have a first kiss in New York City and not have it be in some sort of public location: outside a bar, inside a bar, on the subway platform. Didn't think the MTA experience could possibly get any worse? Well, now you have to watch me make out on the NQRW platform, suckers!

This problem is just going to get worse as the Earth gets more and more crowded until we all have only four square feet to ourselves. So based on many years of experimentation and shame, here are some acceptable and nonacceptable PDA locations.

Acceptable and Nonacceptable PDA Locations

Acceptable: outside of a bar. This is why they invented the outside of bars. Otherwise it would immediately go from bar to road.

Not acceptable: cab or rideshare. OKAY. I KNOW that EVERYONE LOVES to MAKE OUT IN THE

BACKS OF CABS. I don't do it, but I won't condemn it, mainly because I want to seem hip and cool. I just feel bad that you're subjecting some random person to this intimate moment. You cannot ask your Lyft driver to please roll up the partition in his Prius! You are not Beyoncé.

Acceptable: any sidewalk. Again, if it weren't for kissing it would just be road.

Acceptable: near a lake. I mean, depends on how crowded the lake is, but you're in nature! Live a little.

Not acceptable: the subway. (a) Much like cab drivers, we're all here and we exist, too. Even if you are a teen! There are still other people in the world! (b) There are so many germs on the subway—remember that time the Ebola doctor took the L to Williamsburg, *to bowl*? You really need to keep your tongue in your mouth, for health reasons.

Acceptable: outside the subway. You're saying goodbye! Who knows when you'll ever see each other again! Other than when you're pretending not to notice that the other person is standing directly across from you on the other side of the tracks.

Acceptable: outside your house. It's YOUR house (your landlord's house). YOU have to shovel the sidewalk (your landlord has to shovel the sidewalk); you might as well get to kiss on it.

Will They or Won't They

I am somewhat convinced that the near entirety of my romantic neuroses come from watching romantic comedies. Is it worth it, for the circa-1994 sensitive Hugh Grant? Only time and a large-scale poll of my crushes will tell!

The works of Nora Ephron, Richard Curtis, et al., have fucked me up in many insidious ways, but the worst Bad Thing I have absorbed from romantic comedies is the concept of Will They or Won't They.

It definitely makes sense as a narrative concept—movies can't begin and end in the same moment. And it works as a plotline in films that aren't *about* the romance: Jordana Brewster and Paul Walker have a Will They or Won't They in the first *Fast and the Furious*, if memory serves (not entirely sure as the first one came out at least forty-seven years ago). Nic Cage and Diane Kruger have one in *National Treasure* and *National Treasure 2*. They'd have one in *National Treasure 3* if Netflix ever realized what was good for them and hired me to write it! Will They or Won't Theys are especially associated with sitcoms that have a romantic element. There's Sam and Diane on *Cheers*, Jim and Pam on *The Office*, Nick and Jess on *New Girl* (as my friend Hallie once said, there really does not need to be any new content about two straight white people falling in love). Nothing keeps people coming back for about five seasons too long like the chance that two professionally hot people will decide to kiss, permanently.

In movies, where there are only ninety narrative minutes to fill as opposed to twenty-two minutes for twenty-two weeks for eleven years, Will They or Won't They is paired with an acute economy of characters. There are maybe four people total in the world of a movie, and our protagonist is bound to end up with one of them. Meg Ryan ends up with Joe or Frank (*You've Got Mail*) or Joe or Harry (*When Harry Met Sally . . .*); we don't get a sense that there are really any other options.

Will They or Won't They teaches us that if your love interest is incompatible with you—if they straight-up reject you, even— well, that's just the beginning of your journey toward love. It means that you have SPARKS (very important) and the initial conflict will just make your one kiss at the end of the movie that much more iconic. (The trope of the lovers kissing just once at the end of the movie, à la Joe Fox and Kathleen Kelly in Riverside Park in *You've Got Mail*, is infuriating to me. I kiss people several times before deciding if I even like them. Dr. Helen Fisher calls this concept "slow love.") All of this sends the message: lovers have long, emotional arcs before eventually settling down in everlasting love. Shakespeare said, "The course of true love never did run smooth," but rom-coms say the same thing about the course of getting around to kissing even once.

The deluded belief that every crush is a possible They Will plays out in two ways. The first, which I mainly associate with men, is being aggressively persistent even after being told no. I have friends who have told men no multiple times, only to have the men continue to pursue them in a way that my friends and I considered stalking. There's a lot of reasons men feel it is okay and normal to do that, and I think a big one is that the stories our culture tells us *for entertainment* say that a woman's no doesn't mean "I am unequivocally uninterested"; it means "convince me." On the off chance that any man made it past the title of this book and men's innate antipathy toward buying books and is reading this now: *no literally means no.* If women want to go out with you, we'll say yes. We're not trying to drag out this story for eleven seasons.

The other Will They or Won't They–influenced behavior pattern, which is more respectful to the crush but which I've realized really demeans the crusher, is spending forever mooning over someone hoping that they eventually have an epiphany that they're in love. So one of my biggest hobbies. I will say that I have had some rom-com-worthy slow burns with guys. There was one guy I didn't kiss until ten years after we met cute (he climbed on top of a giant pile of dirt and punched my brother in the face). But, on the whole, these "I LOVE BLYTHE" epiphanies never come. And then I'm "caught off guard" when, a year into my mooning, the dudes in question suddenly have girlfriends.

I shouldn't be! In real life, there aren't four total characters! These dudes aren't choosing between me and one other girl. They're choosing between me and all 3.8 billion other women on Planet Earth. When I met them, my crushes already knew tons of girls, some of whom they were likely crushing on. Every moment of every day they're meeting potential new crushes. If some dude isn't into me, he's not going to suddenly decide he's into me for lack of options. And the reverse is true—I'm meeting a lot of people all the time, too! My person will probably end up being someone who would just be an extra in the movie version of my imagined great romance with my hopeless crush. He could be one of the other dudes in the background of the scene at the Christmas party where Bridget Jones meets Mark Darcy. There's one who looks pretty cute! I'm 40 percent convinced that he's David Tennant!

Will They or Won't They is fake news. If you like people, just ask them out. Believe their response. Try not to moon. You're not trying to sustain an eight-season sitcom. In fact, live every day like it's the last season of your sitcom. Wrap up those dang story lines!

The Best Rom-Coms of All Time and How They Ruined Me

When Harry Met Sally . . . : Billy Crystal IS NOT FUNNY! Joke cadences are not jokes! Silly voices are sometimes jokes, but when Billy Crystal does them, they're not jokes. Also, not that this ruined me, but I am convinced Billy Crystal does not have a job in this movie.

***Moonstruck*:** I will never love a real-life man as much as I love Nic Cage threatening to kill himself in front of Cher with a Big Knife.

***Much Ado About Nothing*:** I have only very recently realized that mean funny banter is NOT the same as flirting.

***Love Actually*:** It is just as overdone to point out how the Keira Knightley/guy from *The Walking Dead* plotline is very stalkery as it is overdone to point out that "Baby It's Cold Outside" is very rapey. So I will say that I once went on a date with a guy who loved *Love Actually*, and I said, "Ugh, that movie is so problematic." He said, "How so?" and I said, ". . . I forget."

***Pretty Woman*:** Richard Gere is sixty-eight in real life. His wife is THIRTY-FIVE. This is <u>FUCKED UP</u>!!! I wish I could double underline this!!!!

***Bridget Jones's Diary*:** It is absurd that Bridget equivocated for even a second about wearing the giant underwear. Giant underwear is one of my purest joys in life and I will never again feel ashamed of it.

Clueless: After finally watching this movie in 2013 I spent ninety-nine cents at the Apple Store so that every time I got a text my phone would go, "Ugh, as if!" I refused to ever put it on silent, and I lost a lot of friends.

La La Land: Enough think pieces have been written about how this movie is white-supremacist propaganda, so I will just say that Damien Chazelle is exactly the breed of young white Harvard guy that is very triggering to me.

Ruby Sparks: A guy once texted me, "Sometimes I don't know if you're real or if I scripted you, *Ruby Sparks*–style," and at the time I thought it was very sweet.

Breakfast at Tiffany's: I am now always trying to sit on a fire escape singing "Moon River" in a way that I think is charming but is terrorizing to all who hear (mainly my roommates and the guy who goes onto the roof under my window to make loud business phone calls).

Notting Hill: I'm always trying to break into private property.

Before Sunrise: Normalized young men with very, very greasy hair.

How to Lose a Guy in Ten Days: Encouraged me to turn my love life into Content.

Being Mean

In Nora Ephron movies, before falling in love in the last scene, the protagonists spend ninety minutes being mean to one another. How mean? Well, Tom Hanks in *You've Got Mail* refers to himself as "Mr. Nasty." Billy Crystal in *When Harry Met Sally . . .* insults Meg Ryan's choice of career and spits grape seeds on her car window. It's like: leave Meg Ryan alone!

Two hot people in a movie being mean to one another is supposedly "flirting." It shows they're able to banter! They spark emotional reactions from one another! They upend each other's psychic lives and THAT'S WHAT LOVE IS, according to the cinema we let teach us how to live! Meg Ryan as Kathleen Kelly says that the books you read as a child become an integral part of your identity, and since I watched *You've Got Mail* conservatively eight hundred million times as a child, it's part of my identity. This is a problem because Nora Ephron was wrong: Being mean is NOT flirting. Being mean is just being an asshole.

It has taken me my entire young life to learn this. It makes sense why characters in romantic comedies spar before getting together—as I wrote in "Will They or Won't They?," it extends the narrative. And in real life being mean can be fun; there's a thrill in realizing you're able to come up with a barbed retort on the fly. (To be clear, mean flirting is different from "negging," a legitimately sociopathic pick-up artist tactic where men say shitty things to women to try to lower the woman's self-esteem enough that the woman would consider sleeping with these horrible, pathological dudes. Being mean as a flirt is two-sided and involves "bons mots.")

I bought into mean flirting for many years. I had become Bad. My friends called me Bad Blythe. But after a while I thought about it and realized that any time I've actually had a nice time with a man over a sustained period, that man was never mean to me, even in a flirty way. Unlike a ninety-minute movie, an actual relationship is not meant to be a long-term stress ball. It's supposed to be joyful! Being genuinely sweet to cute boys has been thrilling for me. Instead of nervously keeping up a difficult tonal balance of rude and cute, a dude and I will just watch *Hunt for the Wilderpeople*. It's a lot more relaxing, and the guy from *Jurassic Park* is in it!

Me being mean doesn't make me hot, and (it took me longer to realize) men are never hot BECAUSE they are mean. Take Morrissey. Morrissey is physically hot, he's a creative genius, but he's a nightmare. The fact that he's got a lot of internal issues that he's displacing on other people does not ADD to the hotness. It exists next to it, and arguably detracts. Morrissey needs to take a chill pill, and then Morrissey needs to give me a call!

Sometimes I'll be on the phone with my mom, telling her about the banal details of my life—I was in the edit of a show until three A.M., and one of the producers got snappy and yelled at me for no reason—and out of nowhere my mom will tell me, "Don't marry a man like that, Blythe." Usually I'm like, WHY ARE YOU TELLING ME THIS and THAT DUDE IS JUST MY FRIEND and AGH, MOM, YOU'RE EMBARRASSING ME and ULTI-MATELY YOU'VE JUST REMINDED ME I AM MOTORCY-CLING THROUGH THIS LIFE FOREVER ALONE, SIDECAR FILLED WITH ONLY SADNESS, but: my mom makes a great point. People don't suddenly get un-mean as soon as you stop find-ing that meanness invigorating. They stay mean, and then you're married to them. It wears you the fuck down, like an angry river that just thought of an admittedly funny but acutely hurtful com-ment about something dumb the riverbed just did.

I've learned my lesson. While I'm still unable to be attracted to anyone without a British accent, I'm able to be attracted to people who are purely kind to me. And I knew I internalized this when watching *The Force Awakens*, I saw Kylo Ren and thought to my-self, "Don't marry a man like that, Blythe."

Hello, It's Mr. Nasty: Definitive Proof That Tom Hanks's Character Is the Villain of *You've Got Mail*

You've Got Mail *is a romantic story about a charming, funny busi-nessman who falls in love with a bookstore owner, despite initially clashing in person—or so Warner Bros. wants you to think! (And FYI . . .* You've Got Mail *is one of my favorite movies!! Don't hate* *the player [*You've Got Mail*], hate the game [white-supremacist cap-italist patriarchy].)*

1. Tom Hanks (Joe Fox) writes a flirty email complaining about people ordering complicated coffee drinks

. . . but the example he gives is TALL DECAF CAPPUCCINO. This is a standard, low-maintenance order; the only modifier is decaf, and as modifiers go that is pretty boring. "He probably hates cappuccinos," says you, wrongly. EARLIER IN THE MOVIE he and business subordinate/friend-for-hire Dave Chappelle bro out about how "We're going to seduce [Fox Books customers] with our square footage, and our discounts, and our deep armchairs, and . . ." *IN UNISON* "Our cappuccino!"

2. Tom Hanks takes all the caviar from some weird savory cake blob dish (??) at a party.

That caviar is a GARNISH! Tom Hanks feels that he is entitled to the whole world. He is a real boob! Meanwhile Meg Ryan, while admittedly being emotionally unfaithful to her partner, is overall an orb of pure joy. Something to consider: twenty years post–*You've Got Mail*, Tom Hanks is universally beloved and considered "America's Dad," while Meg Ryan is barely working and getting shit from magazines about her plastic

surgery. When it's not like she invented patriarchy!
Just a thought.

3. Parker Posey is supposedly the villain of this movie?

Growing up, I believed Parker Posey was the villain
of this movie (even though she is one of TWO
partners standing in the way of our OTP . . . ?).
However, in recent years I have discovered that
Parker Posey in *You've Got Mail* is just a more
successful version of me. She is brilliant, vital,
energetic, and generous. When asked how she
sleeps at night, she offers a detailed and hard-won
sleeping pill recommendation. She, off the dome,
offers Frank a genuine compliment about his
work. Meanwhile, Tom Hanks pays no attention
to anyone else's work and is a cis-het dullard.

3a. Reasons Tom Hanks gets mad at Parker Posey in this movie:

- She shares details of her job and her life.
- She reminds him about a dinner he
  agreed to go to, as her partner.
  - He says: "Can't I just give money
    instead?" (Capitalist: bad)
  - He says: "What is it this week? Free
    Albanian writers?" (Unconcerned
    with genocide, maybe racist?: bad)

- She talks about Julius and Ethel Rosenberg.
- She decides to offer Meg Ryan a job.
- She says that if she ever gets out of the elevator she's stuck in, she'll get her eyes lasered.
- She inquires about the location of her Tic Tacs.

3b. If Tom Hanks hated Parker Posey so much.

- He should have broken up with her.
- Instead of stringing her along until he could find somebody better.

4. Tom Hanks speaks condescendingly to the Latina cashier at Zabar's.

Tom Hanks: Hi.

TH: Rose.

TH: That is a great name, Rose.

[points out credit card machine]

TH: This is a credit card machine.

TH: Happy Thanksgiving.

TH: It's your turn to say "Happy Thanksgiving" back.

[does aggro knock-knock joke]

5. Tom Hanks loves *The Godfather.*

I would let this slide if it weren't for the fact that
Tom Hanks (A BOOK SCION) has apparently
never heard of *Pride and Prejudice.* This is
because Tom Hanks has never read a book by a
single woman or a person of color. Additionally,
Tom Hanks believes that all books written by
women should have pink covers and titles written
in curly fonts.

6. Tom Hanks catfishes Meg Ryan for all of act three.

Tom Hanks knows that Meg Ryan is his internet
crush, but she doesn't know that he is hers, and
so he toys with her for a solid couple months.
We are meant to think this is romantic, but in
actuality it is fucked up. Also, at the end, Tom
Hanks brings his dog when he "meets" Meg
Ryan for the first time. This is a contentious
opinion but personally I do not want a dog
jumping all over me while I kiss someone, and
YES, I AM talking from experience.

7. Tom Hanks is a privileged white man.

While he probably thinks he "worked hard"
for his wealth, Tom Hanks in *You've Got Mail*
is at LEAST third-generation rich. He is an

unconflicted capitalist who laughs when
small businesses fail. In my opinion his character
would be appointed to a cabinet position in the
Trump administration or, BEST-case scenario,
have a lot to say about HRC writing a memoir.

Romantic Friendship

Lauren Graham once referred to Matthew Perry as a "Friend Who
I Almost But Never Exactly Dated." I feel in my heart that she is
describing a romantic friendship. It's a friendship that you know,
know, KNOW has a romantic element, but is somehow not evolving to dating. You're just friends, but at the same time everything
is way too intense for it to be entirely platonic. The defining
feature of romantic friendships, maybe, is that THIS SHIT IS
FRAUGHT. I've had many romantic friendships, including one
who basically the entire breakup chapter of this book is about.
AND WE DIDN'T DATE. We kissed once! This, I guess, is why
God invented therapy.

Romantic friendships are different from "the friend zone," a
thing invented by men who think all women owe them sex. This
is a friendship where you could theoretically date (like, you're
each attracted to the other's gender) and you *perform* dating without actually dating. Usually it leaves one or both parties feeling
bad and/or guilty. It's stressful every single second. Mindy Ka-
ling and B.J. Novak have this kind of relationship, I think. She

describes it as "weird as hell." I describe it as "extremely trigger-ing to me."

Some constituent elements of romantic friendships: hanging out all the time, especially at night. I look back at my iCal from romantic friendship periods, and it's all that one dude from ten P.M. to two A.M., four weeknights in a row. And, again, WE ONLY KISSED ONCE, after a year of this. Another element: cuddling. Maybe even sleeping in the same bed, something Lena Dunham calls "platonic bed sharing" and rightly identifies as a horrible idea. My romantic friend and I did this, and now it kills me to know that he is the only man I've been able to fall asleep next to. It makes me feel that I may never be happy again! Maybe I'm just being dramatic because I'm exhausted, but it's true!

Romantic friendships are not a new dumb thing invented by millennials that, somehow, must trace back to the failure of Reagan's economic policy. They've been around for minimum hundreds of years. Take Ginevra de' Benci, the subject of one of legitimately only, like, fourteen paintings Leonardo da Vinci fin-ished in his entire lifetime (MEN FAIL UPWARD). The painting was commissioned by a man named Bernardo Bembo, Venice's am-bassador to Florence—a man who was *openly* just friends with Ginevra. According to da Vinci biographer Walter Isaacson, Bembo already had a wife and mistress but "struck up a proudly Platonic relationship with Ginevra that made up in effusive adoration what it likely lacked in sexual consummation." Apparently this type of romantic friendship was considered poetic at the time, in that people WROTE POEMS ABOUT IT. Everyone in the Renaissance was a lunatic and thrived on drama. Had I lived then I would have either had a heart attack in the first forty-five minutes or ruled all of Florence with my cadre of fake boyfriends.

The millennial version of romantic friendships has an added layer, which is: many millennial men treat the women they sleep with badly and treat their friends much better. How badly did my main romantic friend treat women? Well, the term "softboy" was literally coined about him. He would show me nudes other women had sent him and read me their sexts, without their or my consent. Once, he told a woman he wanted to officially date her, and then days later slept with someone else. And still, through all of this, I was so into him!

Eventually he told me he couldn't sleep with me because he liked me too much, which I viewed as a really shitty lie. All I could fixate on was the fact that he was sleeping with every other woman in Brooklyn but considered me too gross, I guess? But maybe there was truth to what he was saying, for him at least. Maybe hookup culture has taught us to be chill and dismissive about sleeping with people in a way that's hard to do with people you respect. Maybe to hook up with someone you're friends with, you basically have to be certain that you want to marry them! Because, when we all just ghost each other and unfollow each other on Twitter and move on, in order to enter into something with someone you have to be okay with eventually being a complete and total assholier to them.

I suppose it's possible to have a romantic friendship in which neither party feels bad, or both parties feel bad, but in my experience it has been just one of us, and it has always been me. I've been demonstrably and maybe tragically into the guy, and the guy has fed off it and encouraged it. Maybe subconsciously? But I doubt it? Also in my experience, my true, nonromantic friends (both male and female) have told me, "That guy is bad," and I have said, "No, we're just friends." (Though, and this is true, my friends have said, "That guy is bad," of, without exception, EVERY SINGLE GUY I HAVE EVER BEEN INTERESTED IN. So maybe this is more of a me problem.)

You can't just wait around for these guys to have an epiphany or for your feelings to fade naturally. It's scientifically impossible for feelings to fade when you're cuddling and watching Brainy Horror Movies four nights a week. The only ways out of romantic friendships that I have found are (1) to communicate directly how you feel—a trite suggestion at this point, I know—or (2) to move across the country. The second option is much less scary but works only a couple of times before you've got fake boyfriends in every port. Option one almost certainly leads to rejection, because if your romantic friend really wanted you, they would have already acted on your obvious feelings. But telling your friend about your feelings breaks the spell. You know definitively how they feel, and you can move on with your life, with or without them in it. Sometimes these men really aren't feeding off the attention you're giving them, and it's possible to be direct about your feelings, get rejected, suffer through a little weirdness, and then get back to being friends. I've done that; it was super strange for a bit and now I'm staying at his house when I see Paul Simon in June. Which, honestly, is better than dating.

Blah Blah Blah "My Girlfriend"

Usually I won't realize something wasn't a date until we get to the end of the night and a guy either (a) says, "Okay, which direction is your subway?" and then hugs me and pushes me on my way; (b) says, "Okay, well, my bus is over there," and then hugs me and pushes me in the opposite direction; or in very rare and confusing cases (c) walks me to my door, ignores my attempt to kiss him, hugs me, and runs away. Sometimes I'll try to salvage this but I have only ever been successful in getting a second, longer, awkwarder hug. One time a guy followed me on Instagram after. Still didn't count as a date.

When this is how I realize that what I thought was a date in fact wasn't a date, it obviously blows, but I get to be embarrassed about it alone. Over ten thousand hours of practice I have developed an It Wasn't a Date ritual, where I don't wash my face because *w h o caaaaares* and where I throw my purse and all my clothes on the floor and just plop into bed. It's partly about having my boobs out in a Kitty-from-*Arrested-Development* "Say goodbye to THESE" way and partly because I'm too lazy to put on PJs. I wake up in the morning refreshed and eager for whatever dates the new day will bring.

The FLIPPING WORST is realizing it isn't a date when, an hour into drinks that are going *very well*, I ask a guy about his romantic history and he tells me the whole story leading up until NOW AND HIS CURRENT GIRLFRIEND. It's like the episode of *Sex and the City* where Carrie and Berger go on a great date-that-isn't-explicitly-a-date, and when she invites him to her book launch party he says he can't because his girlfriend's parents are going to be staying with them that day. In the split second that they say "girlfriend," you feel so embarrassed and so naive and stupid but also you have to focus really hard on making sure your face doesn't betray that you ever thought this was anything other than friendly drinks. And then you're like, "What does a human face look like? Am I remembering to smile with my eye muscles? Is it possible to fake that? What if he knows how to read microexpressions?"

But you SHOULDN'T feel dumb. It's not your fault. It is the responsibility of the partnered person to clarify any date ambiguity, *in advance* of the nondate. Because: just because someone is partnered doesn't mean that he isn't capable of vibing on you. And just because someone is a nice beta male doesn't mean he isn't capable of being shady.

("But what if he's nonmonogamous." He should still have mentioned that he has a nonmonogamous girlfriend before the date! If you want to be sisterwives, awesome, and if you don't: that is also legal!)

In retrospect, I'm incredibly grateful to have had the following humiliating experience, or I might have gone my whole life thinking *I* was the idiot when men who are Objectively Flirting With Me mentioned late in the game that they had a girlfriend:

I went to a party where I knew only the host. The person I knew next-best was someone who I had met and exchanged four total sentences with several years before, and so I ended up in a corner of the kitchen talking to him. I didn't have high hopes for the conversation, because three of the total sentences we had exchanged were me giving him compliments and the fourth was him going "Okay" and walking away. But I ended up talking to this guy almost the entire time I was at the party, for at least two hours straight. (Usually while telling this story I say it was three, for effect.) It was definitely VERY LONG ENOUGH that even I, a woman incapable of giving or receiving signals, could tell that this guy was vibing on me.

But then, at some point in the conversation, I think after he made a selfie gif of us but before he asked for my phone number, he mentioned that he had a girlfriend who lived across the country. They were at that time, or had been at a time immediately previously, on a break. I'm not sure of the details because as soon as I heard the word "girlfriend" I hit the ejector button on that particular plane ride and parachuted down into a field of "How do I extricate myself from this conversation and this party?" I love women, a gender which is not oppressing me, and I am not trying to cause any anonymous woman problems. So I did leave the party, and I went on with my life, and even after the guy texted me that selfie gif the next day I figured that he had a girlfriend and that I was imagining he was into me.

BUT! THEN! Months later! During a three-hour period when I had Bumble, I got a text from this guy with a screenshot showing we had matched, and the comment "What have we done?" His relationship had ended, and he and I hooked up a couple times before he dumped me on a subway, kissed me again, and ultimately dumped me again via text. It was all worth it, though, for vindication that he WAS into me at that party! I was NOT IMAGINING IT! (And also worth it because he is a kind, smart, interesting dude and now we are friends blah blah blah blah blah.)

So anyways: sometimes you meet people in group settings who seem to be into you, and when you're not stuck near a spice rack talking to them for three to seven hours straight, it might not come up that they have a girlfriend. That's fair, it happens. And then sometimes you ask those people out for a drink via Instagram DM. That's also fair! Good for you, honestly, for putting yourself out there.

I know I wrote a chapter ago that I don't think we can find our way to a unified definition of a date—but whatever you, personally, would mean by "Let's go on a date," I think you should mean the same by "Let's get a drink." Please, we're adults, let's make one thing in this wretched life easy on one another!! Let's agree that "Let's get a drink" is asking someone on a romantic date! You are asking them to drink alcohol with you. That's not even an activity. That's like saying "Let's kill time for a couple hours and then kiss." Listen, I know that sometimes attractive adults get drinks to network. Congress: if we cannot outlaw networking with men, let's at least pass a law saying you have to keep it to caffeinated drinks at establishments that close at nine P.M.

Sure, there's a way that this dude could, through great force of willful ignorance, CONSTRUE "getting drinks" as you making an overture toward friendship, but past a certain age, I and most people I know are not really in the market for new friends. We've already caught enough in our Poké Balls through sixteen-plus years of schooling, through multiple jobs, and through improv classes at three separate theaters in Chicago and two in New York. We're old enough that we're getting more responsibility at work, going to weddings every weekend, and finally embracing the fact that it is NORMAL to need ten hours of sleep a night, at LEAST. We're stressed about how infrequently we get to see the friends we already have and love. Stephen Thomas at *Hazlitt*, citing a study by British researchers, has written that "On average, both men and women start to lose friends around age twenty-five, and continue to lose friends steadily for the rest of our lives." It sucks, obviously. But this is why none of our parents have friends. "That's not true," you say. "My mom has two friends." EXACTLY.

So while I continue to meet new people, and some of those people do become my friends, I'm really not trying to make new friends and I'm especially not trying to make male friends. Female friends understand all the patriarchal bullshit I have to deal with. They more readily consent to talk to me about *Riverdale*. And I already have too many male friends, from going on too many ambiguous dates with them and being tricked into emotionally investing in their lives.

The only male friend I am actively looking for right now is one I can love. If you already have someone you love, I'd like you to save me the time and embarrassment of going on a nondate with you.

I genuinely get that no one wants to be the dick who is like, [raises megaphone to lips] "I HAVE A GIRLFRIEND," while meanwhile the barista is like, "I was just asking your name so I could write it on your tall decaf cappuccino." But better to casually and pseudo-organically make clear your partnered status before the date than to mention it after an hour of flirting, and even then only when directly questioned. The latter just makes me feel simultaneously stupid and put on standby for when you and your girlfriend break up. Which—probably would not make your girlfriend very happy.

Listen: SOMEONE needs to make it clear that you have a girlfriend, and since I don't know, it's gonna have to be you. It may not be fun, but you get couples Halloween costumes and emotional support and all the other perks of having a partner. This is the trade-off.

Professionally Insecure Woke Boys

There are certain types of men who you expect to oppress you. These include Republicans, venture capitalists, and men from South Carolina whose friend Gunnar had a horrible time at Fyre Festival. If you choose to date these men and find that they make weird comments to you about your makeup or they dismiss the new Harry Styles album just because H. Styles started out in a boy band or they, like, voted for Trump—well, it's not like there wasn't a hot girl at the beginning of this race waving a big red flag! (Another red flag: guys who love hot girls at the beginning of races waving a big flag.)

I am very vigilant about excluding these kinds of men from my life. One strategy for doing this is rolling my eyes. Men hate this very much and are constantly telling me to stop. It's like that Margaret Atwood quote that men are afraid women will laugh at them, and women are afraid men will kill them: men hate when

I roll my eyes at them, and I hate when men take away my structural power and my reproductive agency.

AND YET.

Even the "good" men who I hang out with, men who have never told me that Bernie would have won if he had been the Democratic candidate, tell me all the time that they could never be with women who are more professionally successful than they are.

For the longest while, I thought that these by most accounts "woke" boys were just quirkily insecure. Like, oh, that's just Jon, he believes brand-name deodorant will kill you and can't be with a woman who is more successful than he is. Or, oh, Floyd, his thing is that he still rides a hoverboard even though it's illegal now and also he's terrified of being with a woman who has a good job. I also wondered if Jon and Floyd were generally fine with the idea of a motivated woman but had been scared off of it by personal contact with me, an ambitious five-hundred-year-old hag who maintains the appearance of a hot twenty-seven-year-old by feeding on the misdeeds of men and turning them into *New Yorker* pieces.

Then, on the evening of November 8 and the morning of November 9, 2016, I watched the world end in slow motion as it became more and more clear that Donald Trump was going to be president. Over the next couple weeks I did a lot of thinking. Were the majority of Americans rooting for me, a woman? (The electoral college was not.) Should I stop trying to make it in comedy and go get a law degree to actually help people, or would I just meet some charming doofus at Yale Law who would convince me to move to

Arkansas, ruining everything? I realized I was going to have to step it up to make sure I was using my privilege to convince other white women to not be flipping racist idiots. I realized I needed to start swallowing IUDs pronto before the Affordable Care Act was repealed. And I also realized—not to put too fine a point on it—that men who say they can't be with more successful women are not being quirkily insecure; they are being straight-up sexist. Professionally Insecure Woke Boys are policing women into not being too ambitious.

There are already so many obstacles to women advancing in the workplace—there's the pay gap, there are old boys' clubs that give men connections that women have no access to, there are the people who for some reason think I need to brush my hair a couple times a month to look "professional"—the list goes on. But even if a woman advances professionally against all odds, she then gets punished by losing access to "that sweet D" (romantic love).

When it's just your one coworker Floyd telling you he can't be with a more professionally successful woman, it's easy to be like, "LOL, okay, Floyd, I think I can survive without access to your D and your hoverboard and your opinions about grammar." But when all of society—INCLUDING the Democrats/socialists/anarchists who you hoped were basically on the side of women—just "feel" that they don't want to be romantically attached to women who are setting short- and long-term goals and achieving those goals, then successful women are losing out on a socially significant amount of D!

There's a level of professional success at which you basically have no choice but to date a man who is less successful than you are. Like Nicki Minaj and Meek Mill. Or Joni Mitchell and Graham Nash. Or Elizabeth Warren and whoever the heck Elizabeth Warren is with (I hope . . . Bradley Whitford). At a certain point, the only D that women have left are the ~über-woke~ Matt McGorrys of the world. And having to date Matt McGorry is the cruelest punishment.

What are individual men thinking when they say they can't be with more successful women? I mean, I fully believe they are saying this because it's a way that our patriarchal society has conditioned them to police ambitious women, but I don't think THEY think about it that way at all.

Maybe these Professionally Insecure Woke Boys just want to feel manly—not like Clint Eastwood but like the bearded lumberjack-type Instagram dudes who live in A-frame houses. Maybe they don't want to feel judged. Maybe they feel like there can be only one star in every partnership, that someone has to be the Nabokov and someone has to be the Véra (or someone the Virginia Woolf and someone the Leonard).

The idea that there is enough space for only one genius in a couple is based mostly on jealousy and insecurity, I suspect. It would probably be nice to have a partner wholly dedicated to helping you realize your best self. It would be just as nice to have a partner whose passion and dedication to their art inspires you and whose successes pull both of you up into the next echelon of whatever field you work in—a romantic version of Aminatou Sow and Ann Friedman's "shine theory." Okay, maybe two ambitions in one partnership (as opposed to one spread over two people) will increase the amount of busyness and harried-ness and stress, but in my opinion all truly successful people have lived in a constant state of stress since about age sixteen. They find happiness not by getting rid of that stress but by finding a way to normalize its existence, and also by moving upstate.

I would guess that men who don't want to feel judged by their partners know deep down that they either don't know what they want to do with their lives, or really DO know what they want to do and it is . . . nothing, to be honest. (And they feel bad about it. There are men who know they want to do nothing and feel GOOD about it and who are very comfortable dating successful women. One of those men recently told me, as a flirt, "I would love to do nothing all day except cook and fuck.") These insecure men feel that having successful partners would throw their lack of direction or ambition into even starker relief. Maybe, having been raised on Kevin James sitcoms, they think more successful wives would nag them about this. To these men, I would say: get over yourselves; and to men who want to seem masculine, I would say: examine the origins and consequences of those urges and meanwhile, go chop a log or something and let me work.

Anyway, as much as men claim to love logical, well-reasoned arguments, I know that no logical argument is ever going to change how men decide which women to smooch. How does that change happen? I THINK it would either be from (a) representations in pop culture or (b) from having a cousin with a more successful female partner. So in lieu of me dating everyone's cousins (I mean, I'm trying), this is my official call to Netflix to hire me to write a sitcom about an ambitious woman happily dating a less successful dude. Right after you hire me to write a third *National Treasure*.

Types of Men Who Are Bad

Men Who Will Be Cured by Love (They Won't)

These are men who are something between active meanies and passive assholes to everyone they meet—think Mr. Darcy, the Beast in *Beauty and the Beast*, or the dude who told me when we met that he was incapable of experiencing human emotion. Despite your best efforts, they will not be cured by love. They will maybe be cured by therapy, but you don't need to stick around to find out.

"Nice Guys"

A "nice guy" is a man who feels it is a huge sacrifice to treat women with human dignity. In actuality this should not require an extraordinary effort and is not in itself deserving of sex.

Devil's Advocates

White men who enjoy playing devil's advocate are latent Republicans. (They say they're progressives, but give them ten to fifteen years.)

Republicans

As the kids say, "don't @ me."

Men Who Use Read Receipts

Read receipts are the single most evil element of phone culture; they exist in this world for the sole purpose of causing pain. Before they were invented you would have had to text, "Just FYI: I saw that you texted me, but I'm not responding because I hate you." The worst burn I ever received was when I texted a guy, "I'm back from vacation! Let's get together and watch National Treasure 2!" and he read it and waited seven hours before texting me just "welcome back."

Types of Men Who Are Great

Actually Nice Guys

These are men who treat you kindly because they are kind, not because they're trying to sleep with you. Cool. Next!

Men Who Come to My Shows

In a world where everyone is obsessed with being busy, spending time with someone is the ultimate flirt. My friend Jose's boyfriend once told him in the early stages of their relationship, "Put me on your schedule," which struck me as tantamount to a marriage proposal. Coming to my shows is an even more forward version of generic "spending time with me," because you're showing up at a place where you know I'll be at an event which is designed to give me validation. Once, a dude came to two of my shows in three days, and I was like, "Oh, he wants to bone." (He did!)

Men Who Are Adam Driver-Hot

Men like Adam Driver are hot, but—as Lena Dunham pointed out—in such a way that every woman feels like she is the only one who has discovered the fact of his hotness. They're not conventionally hot enough to be an action hero, but they're hot enough to be the villain or the techy friend, which ultimately means they're still hot enough to be in a movie. I'm sure most of these men know that they're hot; the ones I consider Good are the ones who are chill about it (Adam Driver, Domhnall Gleeson), not the ones who are assholes (Miles Teller).

Harry Styles

Though I wish Harry would have tweeted about the 2016 presidential election, I overall consider him the ideal progressive rockstar. I am sad that he cut his hair, but I have come to terms with the fact that you can reject toxic masculinity and still have a conventionally masculine haircut. Maybe in actuality Harry is a mess—it is annoying that he is only ever seen on dates with thin, uninterestingly hot women—but the idea of him is very inspiring to me.

Men Who Love Their Moms

No joke here! Get right with your mom!

5

GETTING
SERIOUS

"Defining" the "Relationship"

At what point, and why, do you and the person you're kissing decide to start calling each other boyfriend and girlfriend—to define the relationship?

First, a disclaimer: I actually hate the word "girlfriend"—I don't relate to it at all and am very uncomfortable referring to myself as such. Maybe it's from consuming mainstream pop culture that portrays the girlfriend as an annoying obstacle? Maybe I got tired of referring to myself as a "girl" after referring to myself as a "girl" five hundred thousand times a day during the years that "girl" and "lady" were the cool words to use when describing a woman? (I now refer to myself as an "immortal demon.") But yeah, I hate it. I'm like [crumples up English language, throws in trash]: "This language is bad; we gotta start over." I sometimes say "boyfriends" instead of boyfriend and girlfriend, but have been told recently that it is weird, stupid, and possibly offensive. Then I bought one pair of corduroy bell-bottoms and suddenly love the words "lover" and "partner." It's probably still just as stupid to say "partners" as a straight woman, but is more "learning from queer culture" than "appropriating queer culture." And as my (gay) former roommate Zach says, "Anyone can say partner. Boy/girlfriend is unnecessarily gendered and infantilizing."

I've heard people refer to themselves as boyfriend and girlfriend after two weeks, which I consider bonkers. How is that even possible? You have seen each other maybe twice. Maybe I'm just too busy and it's completely normal for people to see each other multiple times a week in the first weeks of going out. But honestly, I think considering oneself busier than normal is a super narcissistic thing to do and now assume everyone else is exactly as busy as I am. SO WHERE DOES ANYONE GET OFF becoming a couple so quickly? Maybe these people are just extroverts who love going to bars? For me to rearrange my life to see someone multiple times in the first week of knowing them, they'd have to be so perfect that it seemed as if I had dreamed them up. This has happened to me only once, and . . . say it with me . . . WE DIDN'T KISS.

If not after two weeks, do you define the relationship after two months? I have a friend who has been seeing a woman for two months and just had another friend tell him, "You gotta have The Talk soon." He agreed and is working up the courage and stamina. So: two months seems socially acceptable. I'm certainly not against a world in which I meet someone, hook up with them for two months, and decide I want to stop trying to bone other people and start overusing the word "boyfriend" when describing this dude to my friends.

But at press time I have been seeing someone I have yet to call my boyfriend for, generously, over three years on and off. I don't want to be a couple, and I'm 60 percent sure he doesn't want to be either, and for the moment it feels like less trouble to not talk about it. In short, I feel that the timing of defining the relationship is between you, the person you're kissing, and the Holy Ghost.

Let's discuss for a moment, if you will, what you call yourselves in the (possibly infinite) time before you are a couple. Not when you're trying to figure out what you are to each other, but when you're on the same page that you're nonexclusively sleeping with each other fairly regularly, as I am. I HATE the term "friends with benefits." Number one: Sure, this person is my friend, but to the point that basically EVERYONE in the world is my friend: I like them and I spend time with them. In that regard, my family are my friends, my coworkers are my friends, my baristas who don't know my name are my friends. So none of these people are actually my friends, and Americans have diluted the word "friend" to meaninglessness. Number two: "Benefits"?! What a gross, corporate way to describe sex! Are we all having sex in our suits, briefcase in hand? And does that mean that our normal friendships have no benefits? Of course, "hooking up" is not much better—it has kind of a fratty, emotion-free, "We're all young and hot and banging everybody [three Caucasian 'rock on' emoji]" connotation. And while I certainly sleep with people without wanting to date them, I'm still a human experiencing emotions for them! Also, when I refer to someone as my "hookup partner," it is always so jarring that whoever I am talking to stops the conversation and says, "I have never heard anyone say such a thing before." In summary:

precoupledom, I basically just refer to people I'm kissing as my "friend," and it's slowly driving me to madness.

Anyway: at a certain point do you become a common-law couple, even without formally discussing it? Is it after you spend a certain amount of time being exclusive? Does it matter if you weren't sleeping with other people, but not for lack of trying? Does hanging out on Valentine's Day automatically mean you are dating? (I know it's the most clichéd thing in the world to complain about Valentine's Day forcing a "define the relationship" conversation, but regardless I found it stressful and have filed suit against the Hallmark corporation.) If I see a person every week, if I ask about his family, if our families know one another exist, if we respect each other a lot, and maybe most importantly, if I never stress out about how often I'm texting him: Are we dating? What's the law here? Why has this never been on an episode of *Suits*?

And what if we were hooking up with other people—does that make us common-law polyamorous? Or do you have to intentionally decide to be polyamorous and then tell everyone you know to read *The Ethical Slut* for it to count? I definitely have nothing against seeing multiple people and enjoyed it for the about two weeks I managed to make it work, once. But just like officially calling someone your boyfriend involves a narrowing down of possibilities and an announcement that this is the kind of person you are and the kind of person you love, deciding to identify as polyamorous is making a big declaration about yourself that I am not interested in doing. I'd rather just slink around the edges of things like a Rumpelstiltskin of kissing, trying to avoid having a name thrust on me, thus ruining everything and forcing me to give back all these babies.

Do you owe it to someone to define your relationship? After a certain point, is it cruel not to refer to someone as your boyfriend? Refraining from calling someone your boyfriend makes the eventual breaking up easier and therefore maybe implies you intend to break up with them at some point. It also manages expectations: it doesn't mean you *won't* go to their friends' random parties or attend family weddings with them; it just means you aren't *definitely* doing those things. You could, of course, be a couple and have an understanding that those things aren't expected. You could even be a couple and explicitly be comfortable with the idea that you may one day break up. I have had married friends who have told me they would never have gotten married if they didn't feel comfortable with one day being divorced. But by not labeling yourself a couple, you make it clearer that you aren't on the path to some other, more serious label (like "a married couple"). You're not contextualizing your relationship to other people. If you're both comfortable with that, and with the extra five minutes it takes to explain your exact relationship status to your mom, who is cooler than you think and also probably doesn't care . . . I don't think it's cruel.

Just keep in mind that by not calling yourselves a couple, you're also not contextualizing your relationship to yourself. We're on the cusp of so many societal shifts: the way the economy works, the kinds of jobs people have, the age at which people "settle down," the kinds of things women are allowed to do—everything is changing extremely rapidly. Hell, I look at photos of Madewell clothes from a few years ago and CANNOT BELIEVE I ever wanted to pay $130 to dress like a sepia-toned farmhand. The way in which we're dating and loving is changing along with and because of all those other things, and not having a familiar wagon rut to follow is very weird and difficult. At times it feels like the guy I'm kissing and I are inventing human connection as we go along. Calling yourselves a couple, a team, lets you feel like your life has an order; you know what comes next. It's like ordering a preexisting poke bowl off a menu, because even if it has some ingredients you're not in love with, it beats trying to build your own and somehow always ending up with something that costs twenty-two dollars and smells like farts. Being an official couple might come with responsibilities and expectations you don't want, but at least you know what the hell is going on.

Long-Distance

Many of my friends and at least one of my brothers have been in long-distance relationships; I, personally, have never. I'm not opposed to the concept, but the only person I could see myself dating long-distance lives in a different country and has only expressed extremely tepid romantic interest in me for six hours, two years ago, MAYBE.

It seems like the general population—aka people I have talked to and movies I have seen (It's not like I did a longitudinal, representative study of this; I'm not trying to call strangers at home like the creeps at Gallup)—consider long-distance relationships to be in a liminal state. Long-distance relationships are only long-distance while the partners work toward a future in which they live in the same place. Even if that future is extremely nebulous, since you're not really making any concrete steps and also because maybe you think we're all going to die in, like, a chemical nuclear winter due to a massive oil refinery fire before you can figure out how to get a job in Portland, you're working toward it in theory.

Dating long-distance also seems to involve careful planning to make sure you hit some quota of relationship hours per month. I often read about celebrities who make sure not to go longer than two weeks without seeing each other. (It is my office job to read interviews with celebrities talking about how they make their relationship with Orlando Bloom work. I get healthcare for this!) In between these bimonthly visits, I've had friends who Skype with their partners while watching the same movie and eating the same food. But this seems to be just auxiliary, like if you go long enough without being in the same room with someone and smooching them, you might essentially just be very emotionally connected pen pals.

The point of viewing long-distance relationships as liminal, of always trying to resolve the distance, is that the prolonged period apart can cause problems, even when you're hitting that relationship hours quota. Maybe that's the reason why Hollywood marriages where both partners are often working and traveling seem so much more prone to divorce (or maybe actors are narcissists) (or maybe actors are more likely to be in cults that their wives flee) (or maybe we just hear about those divorces more and are more emotionally invested in Hollywood marriages than we are in the marriages of our friends). You can visit for two weekends a month, you can watch *Planet Earth* over Google Hangouts, but you can't re-create the part of a relationship that's just spending a huge amount of time together doing nothing in particular. As my brother told me, if your relationship has any tiny problems, making your relationship long-distance will make those problems obvious, immediately.

So, okay, say you do move to be with your partner. Maybe you're happy to do it! Like, I love living in New York: my friends are here, there are theaters and art galleries, it's one of the maybe two cities where I could ever get a job writing for TV (please hire me to write for TV). But it's also covered in trash, I spend every morning with my head jammed into another commuter's armpit, and I'm paying $1,400 a month for an apartment where water gushes from the sky-light when I shower (???) (I have decided this is worth it and not a big deal). So at a certain point, the presence of someone you love seems like as good a reason to live somewhere as any.

But just as likely you're sacrificing something by moving, since there's a reason you ended up where you're living in the first place. Is it possible to remove yourself from the place where you decided you needed to be and not in some way resent the other person for it? Is Meghan Markle *really* okay giving up her acting career to be with Prince Harry? Does she have such a low opinion of *Suits*? If *Suits* isn't a good show, then why have I spent over one full day of my life watching *Suits*?

When you're not being funded by crown jewels money and you can't just meet up in Botswana for a second date, long-distance relationships seem like [extremely Ben Affleck winning the Oscar voice] a lot of work. But, like, why?! I think there exists a world in which you don't fight the distance, in which you have a permanent long-distance relationship. Maybe your goals (writing for TV) place you geographically far away from your partner's goals (belonging to a small brotherhood sworn to guard the Svalbard Global Seed Vault); I don't believe that makes you automatically incompatible. Take, for example, the marriage of actor Judith Light (which I read about on my free time and earned NO healthcare benefits for). Judith has been married for thirty-two years to a man who lives across a continent from her: he in Los Angeles and she in New York. As Judith told *People* magazine: "I highly recommend it. He loves California, and I would never ask him to leave there and he would never ask me to leave here." They visit each other for months at a time but have no plans to end up together. It makes sense—according to Dr. Helen Fisher AND SCIENCE, distance and infrequency of seeing each other can make the initial spark last longer. And according to Dame Helen Mirren, spending a lot of time apart and giving each other space has kept her marriage happy. No science behind Helen Mirren's thing, but she is hot, so I trust her implicitly! And perhaps not having to constantly worry about "resolving" long-distance relationships makes them more enjoyable for everyone.

The idea of a permanent long-distance relationship is appealing to me, an introvert who needs to spend a lot of time alone, recharging, staring at my pile of books and thinking about how I'm definitely going to die before reading even half of these books.

Living Together

Deciding to live together is considered a big, important step in a relationship: you decide to officially date, you move in together, you get married, you grow old and pay Elon Musk to shoot you into the sun. But what if . . . I don't wanna?!

I understand WHY people live together. Your boyf is ideally one of your favorite people to hang out with, and living with someone means you see them constantly. There are definitely men who I would love to see constantly, for, like, a week. And it's fun to wake up with someone and immediately start hanging out with them!

But, as a person who sometimes just spends five minutes sitting in an empty bedroom at parties to *recharge,* being forced to hang out with anyone all the time sounds horrible to me. Sometimes I just want to head home and know that no one will be there. And living with roommates is different—they're not in your bed, and you don't have to love them. Your roommates don't care that when you sleep you spin around and mumble about the Obamas. This is true—a guy once told me I had talked in my sleep about the Obamas, and honestly I have never been prouder.

There's also something to living alone in a space that you alone pay for and you alone have earned, feeling proud of yourself as you look around and say, "Look at all my shiiiiiit." And if you want to hang exclusively illustrations by your friend Hallie Bateman, you're allowed to do it, even if your boyfriend thinks that you should hang brown art from the 1970s because brown art is very genius. (He is wrong, no matter how hot he is.)

In an ideal world where we're all rich and there's no housing crisis, I'd love to live fifteen to sixty minutes away from my hot long-term partner. Every night we spent together would feel like a choice, instead of a default setting due to a choice we made three years ago when both of our leases were up at the same time. We'd hang out a lot, but I wouldn't spend every commute home praying that he was in a good mood. And when my period was so bad that I'm changing tampons every hour, I would lock my doors and refuse to let him in!

At the same time: I've lived alone for a while now, and it hasn't solved every single problem in my entire life. My ceiling has one new little crack every day and my Wi-Fi randomly stops working when I'm in the middle of watching an episode of *The Great British Bake Off*, and now those problems belong to me alone. I think I'd probably cave pretty easily on living together, especially if that means I can afford to live somewhere where all the floorboards meet up and none of them are rotting. BUT: I'd like my own bedroom. (Again, in this scenario, we're all rich. But not as rich as those villains who have their own separate *wings*.) I've read enough features in *Parade* magazine to know that having your own space can save a marriage. I'll hang up my illustrations and sit in silence and every single night I'll spin and spin and spin like the corpse of a Founding Father who just learned about Trump.

Negotiables

There are a lot of Important Decisions to be made with a partner, if you've decided you like each other enough to be in it for the long haul. Where do you live? Do you get married? Do you have kids? Are you religious? Are you religious for the kids? Are you VEGAN for the kids? (See: *Eating Animals*, the book Jonathan Safran Foer wrote to trick me into going vegan without doing it himself.)

To these questions, I and many of my friends are like: Ehh, whatever. I'll see how my partner feels. Like I wrote in the long-distance section: I'm very happy in New York, but if I fell in love with someone who had a good reason for wanting to live somewhere else, he could probably convince me! Everywhere's interesting: tell social media that you're traveling to any place on Earth, and you'll get some great recommendations. (Any place except Salt Lake City, a city where, apparently, no one I have ever met has ever been, and I was forced to wander around asking young-looking people what was cool.) (They all said the mall.) (And actually, it *was* a pretty cool mall.)

I have friends who don't particularly believe in marriage but who assume they'll do it one day to please their partner, or their partner's family. Same for having kids, and for religion: I was raised Catholic and don't really believe in anything (although mama does love a crystal), but I'd happily convert to Judaism for a dude because, sure, why not. Does it mean you aren't a feminist if you're willing to leave so much up to a man to potentially help decide?

No, I think! There are some people who feel very strongly about marriage and religion and kids, and honestly congrats to them for being up-front and honest about those things! Multiple friends of mine have ended relationships lately because one partner definitely wanted kids at some point (or now) and one definitely didn't ever (or at least not now). It's such a sucky reason to have to break up a relationship that's otherwise working, but it's a legitimate and fundamental problem! And honestly: I'm still wrapping my head around the fact that friends of mine are old enough to be having kids *on purpose*. I'm not even twelve years old! What the hell is happening?!

Taking into consideration what your partner wants doesn't seem weak or antifeminist to me, as long as your partner is equally open to taking into consideration things that you feel strongly about. And honestly: there are so many problems in the world and so many fights to pick over things you actually feel strongly about. NO, I will never see *Manchester by the Sea*. NO, I will never marry a Republican. And honestly, YES, I am probably going to be an absolute lunatic and when I have a hypothetical child that I don't even know if I want I'm probably going to insist on raising them vegetarian! Deal breakers *do* exist. But if you don't really care about something, and it would make someone you love happy, I think why not go for it. Have an adventure. Most of everything in human history was barely planned and probably a mistake anyways. When my mom found out she was pregnant with me, she sat down and cried. But who cares! Now I'm here and I call her every four hours to tell her about weird scratches and bruises on my body. Life's all chaotic, and it's great.

Marriage Is Bad and I Am for Sure Going to End Up Married to the First Person Who Asks Me

Say what you want about living in the twenty-first century—for example, I feel horrible so constantly that I recently said "I feel bad ALL THE TIME" as a flirt—but one nice thing about the present is that we as a society have started recognizing that the institution of marriage has problems. As is true for things like football and Sean Penn, I dislike marriage for political and sociological reasons. And yet there's a bit of me that still wants to get married! I want to get married in the same way that people want to do the saltine challenge: when I read that women end up trapped in their marriages, I'm like, "Well, it doesn't seem that hard to eat eight saltines in a minute, I honestly think I can do it!" I honestly think I will be the one whose body chemistry, mouth hydration, and willpower will disprove the rest of humanity, and I also think I can be the one person who can defy the odds and NOT end up with the man I love oppressing me and causing my early death.

The early death thing is not a joke! It is for real! One (bigly) thing that's so bad about marriage is that there is a huge imbalance in the benefits of marriage for men and women. Namely, that men get a lot of benefits and women don't. According to Elizabeth Gilbert in *Committed*, studies show that married men compared to single men: live longer; accumulate more wealth; do better in their careers; are less likely to suffer from alcoholism, addiction, or depression; are less likely to die a violent death; and report being happier. Now please imagine the hand-clap emoji between every word in the next sentence: all of that is the exact opposite for women. To quote a man I texted this to: "whaaat." Still pulling from Gilbert here: married women make 7 percent less money and are more likely to die a violent death because . . . their husbands kill them. Gilbert (writing in 2010) does note that things have begun to get better and that the imbalance is diminished by factors such as marrying later in life and having a husband who offers to help with chores. Perhaps there is some hope for me, an infamously lazy septuagenarian. But it's still basically a statistical certainty that in many measurable ways, getting married to a man will hurt me.

This benefit imbalance is the reason, probably, that young girls are taught to be so boy crazy in the first place. No woman could logically be persuaded to spend her life cleaning some dude's house, raising his children, and being his live-in therapist, *for free*. If you added up all the unpaid jobs a traditional wife performs, the salary would probably need to be somewhere in the high seven figures, plus an extremely good healthcare package, to even tempt me. And even still I would probably turn the job down because, like working at Goldman Sachs, the hours are too long, the work is too stressful, and the industry is morally suspect. But when narratives from every form of storytelling yet invented by man constantly tell young girls that life is meaningless without love, this completely illogical sacrifice seems justified. (And, truthfully, I would gladly lower my life expectancy if it meant I got to be married to Colin Firth.)

Despite all this, there currently exist a solid three hot dudes who, if they asked to marry me, I would probably say yes. WHY!?! WHAT IS WRONG WITH ME? (Other than the fact that I have never seen *Fast & Furious*.)

Well, to start with, I'm historically a girl who likes to be good at things. In high school I was a straight-A student, I was the president of every club, I placed in a state-wide math competition even though I hated math. My dad, a paid representative of the powerful Math lobby, was like, "You must love math if you are so good at it!" But the thing I loved was the being good at it. And honestly, I still like being good at things! Why shouldn't I?? Do you want me to enjoy being bad at things, you jerk?! Unfortunately, trying to be "good at" relationships means following a course that has been set for us by countless rom-coms and books and ads from the scam diamond industry telling us that "Every kiss begins with Kay." (Joke's on them: I didn't understand that that slogan was a pun until I was *in my twenties*.) So by being a girl who likes to be good at things, I'm basically digging my own grave and waving up at my laughing husband, who is now living longer due to having siphoned the life out of me, his hot wife.

Another reason I want to get married, which is equally another reason that marriage is bad, is that it provides a huge amount of external validation. External validation is something we are all taught to crave from a very early age, and the search for it makes up the entire personality of our current president. Marriage is a massive hit of external validation: someone is putting on a nice suit and hiring a DJ to announce publicly that they consider you interesting and fuckable. And presumably THEY are a person you consider very cool, meaning that suddenly *you* are cool enough to be considered cool by a cool person! Sort of two feet to the left of the external validation thing, but related: by publicly drawing your validation from someone and offering them validation in return, you're making a very bold statement to the world about who you are. Like, this is the kind of gold-plated decorative skull I like (giant, heinous) and this is the kind of partner I like (tall, wears oxford shirts, always smells like cigarettes). All of this makes me feel so icky about love, like it's an illness and the only solution is to become a Buddhist, which must be why Leonard Cohen went to live on a mountain. BUT! In my heart, I think I'm overintellectualizing it. There's a way to experience love joyfully, remember? It's not bad to really, really, existentially enjoy hanging out with and boning someone.

Also, and I know this makes me a loser: I want romantic stability. I don't want the subversive rom-com; I essentially just want the rom-com. I'm consistently extremely exhausted due to low levels of either vitamin B_{12} or vitamin D_3 (or both?), and the thought of figuring out my partner and just deciding that's that, and we can deal with whatever issues come but I can't trade in for another one: it sounds very appealing. Part of my love for my family and closest friends is, I think, the inevitability: they have always been in my life and always will be and even when we argue so much I sob or when we drive twenty-four hours straight and I don't want to talk to them for two months, we're in it for the long haul and we both know we're going to figure it out. I think I'd like that feeling with a romantic partner. It's hard to make a romantic relationship work for a long time, but it's maybe a little more likely that we'll stay together if we promise to do it in front of all our friends and have to drag our asses to the courthouse to fill out paperwork because of it. It's the sunk cost fallacy, working in favor of love! It would be nice to be illogical in the name of a beautiful thing for a change, instead of to justify playing *Minesweeper* for fifteen more minutes because I've already been playing for thirty so I might as well play until I win. I do think with romantic partners, since you do get to consciously CHOOSE, it's more acceptable to say, "This isn't working, I want out." Which is very clearly a good thing, and necessary. But I also honestly believe we're not entitled to be supremely happy at every moment, and it's not worth it to seek out constant extreme happiness. Don't believe me? Go spend three months reading *Infinite Jest*! Or just take my word for it and spend those three months going on a road trip or something.

Another reason I would totally consent to getting married that has nothing to do with being in everlasting love with any particular guy: cool families. In the last year or so I've started to find that I'm very attracted to men's families. I haven't met any of the families—some of them belong to men who are just crushes— but whenever I see these dudes, I'm like: "How's your mom?" I *love* when people have interesting parents. Your mom's a lawyer? Your dad went back to school while raising young kids? Let's all get brunch! And it's not just parents! I want to hang with everyone. Your brother is a journalist? Your sister owns a rustic farm? Your brother-in-law forces everyone to play cornhole at every family gathering? YOU HAVE AN ADORABLE BABY NIECE, WHO YOU ARE GOOD WITH?! I've always found it attractive when men love their moms, because it's reassuring to know that they can be nice to at least one woman. But the "extremely inter-ested in your family" thing is a new biological/maturation stage, as I get older and theoretically closer to serious commitment. I love my curvy family, and because my parents are divorced I al-ready have to split my time at holidays. I'm now subconsciously shopping for families that would be worth splitting my time even further. And I've already found at least four. SOMEONE MARRY ME!

I also know that my dad really wants me to get married. I've known this forever—my parents are divorced, and whenever I've talked about not being interested in marriage he takes it person-ally, like his divorce is the only reason I'm not interested in lowering my life expectancy and job prospects in one fell swoop. Then, last year, I found out my dad has been saving money for my eventual wedding. I'd of course prefer to have that money to orchestrate many small bribes or to amass gemstones and precious metals, but my dad is not hearing it. None of this was particularly convincing to me, until my dad and I recently went to Disney World. (If you believe it is uncool for adults to go to Disney, here is my response: Andrew Garfield does it.)

For the first, like, eleven hours we were there, my dad just made the same jokes and talked about the same things he always does: Auburn University, his alter ego "Leo," and how the fact that we had FastPasses meant that mathematically we were having a bet-ter time than everyone else. But, later in the day, while waiting in line for It's a Small World, he ran out of his normal things and sud-denly started telling me stuff I had never heard before. Like: "Your mom was the one who wanted that dog we had." And: "I didn't like the name Blythe, but then I saw your mom go through labor and I thought, *Yeesh. You can do whatever you want.*"

And then he told me about being diagnosed with cancer around the time I was born. He told his oncologist, "I have to live long enough to walk my daughter down the aisle." Which is like: JESUS CHRIST. My dad's *one wish* when he was basically my age and diagnosed with cancer was to walk me down the aisle. It makes my "I'm an independent woman who doesn't believe in marriage and never brushes her hair" rhetoric seem a bit selfish. Even though obviously it isn't; I'm leading my own life! But in the Disney World moment, I felt like finding *someone* and marrying them was the only kind thing to do.

Society is on the edge of something new and radical in the way that relationships are organized. But it feels impossible to see how it's going to resolve itself, what's a normal way to act in relationships, and how to be happy at all. It's becoming more and more clear we don't have to plan our lives as a road toward marriage. But then what are we doing? All arcs we thought we were following have been totally overthrown. We have to really tune ourselves in to our desires, which are of course covered by layers of capitalist grime from narratives and advertising. Anything goes, homies! So my new plan is marry the first rich person who asks me, convince a bunch of my friends to move to New Mexico, and die.

BREAKING UP

Love Is Fake

Breakups suck ass, obviously. It's never fun to get told "you deserve better" on a crowded subway or to get texted that your partner has started seeing someone else or to have to tell someone that after agonizing about it you think you need some space, and then have to tell them five hundred more times before you follow through with it. It's in these moments when I'm feeling like shit about myself and the entire world that I like to ask: Is romantic love ultimately a total sham?!

Whenever the question is "Why does all of society believe in this thing which doesn't actually exist and is maybe also bad," the answer is usually that the fake thing serves the purposes of preserving the status quo of capitalism/patriarchy/white supremacy, etc. It's become so necessary to maintaining power structures that benefit a select few that it has become woven into our idea of reality, like *The Matrix,* I assume, since I've never seen *The Matrix,* and also a lot of men's rights activists seem to cite *The Matrix* on Reddit, so maybe I'm completely wrong here.

But it's very apparent why an idea of sustained and passionate romantic love is good for capitalism. It sold greeting cards to olden-times people and now sells, I guess, premium Bitmoji? It sells chocolate, which is completely unnecessary because I would have bought that chocolate anyway. It sells diamond engagement rings for exorbitant prices, even though diamond engagement rings have only been a thing for a century and diamonds are just (not particularly rare) weird-looking rocks. It sells rom-coms where couples say "I love you" after only ninety minutes, which should be illegal. And it's even more apparent how the construct of sustained romantic love enforces patriarchy. It tethers women to men long enough for the woman to legally tie her life and finances to the man. This was especially useful back when divorces were impossible to get and when men were outside plow-farming all day.

The only problem with this very good theory is that the vast majority of people are going to experience the feeling of "love" in their lives. We might not be able to agree exactly on what that word means; love, like pain, is subjective. Some sufferers of chronic pain grit their teeth through each day, while my stepdad sprawls on the couch crying out to Millie and Bailey, a cow and a cat from a computer game my little brother used to play, whenever he has a slight cold. But while we can't be sure that what we're feeling is exactly the same or exactly as intense as what other people are feeling, it seems pretty clear that love is a real thing that exists.

But is love sustainable? Is "happily ever after" real, or was it invented by a Grimm brother who got tired of writing about two conventionally attractive white people falling in love and so decided to end the story right after they kissed for the first time. Well, after they kissed and at least one evil stepsister's eyes got pecked out by birds (the Grimm brothers were demented).

After a lot of reading, living life, talking to friends, and sitting around at family parties just looking at people, I've come to believe that romantic love is a real and true thing that exists in the world but usually lasts for several years as opposed to a whole lifetime.

Anecdotal evidence isn't data, but my parents are divorced, and the parents of almost everyone I know are divorced. It's to the point that when I meet someone whose parents are together, I GASP and then ask if the fact that their parents are together stresses them out.

I hate evolutionary biology—I think it's mostly the science of choice for sexist, racist dickdarts who want to use "evolution" to prove that women don't KNOW how to read, could NEVER know how to read, and therefore shouldn't work at Google. BUT at the same time, evolution is real and maybe can be helpful if we're not using it to oppress people who aren't white men. All that said, biological anthropologist Dr. Helen Fisher observes in *Anatomy of Love* that (a) in hunting-gathering societies, women tend to give birth every three to four years and (b) the modern worldwide divorce peak is after three to four years of marriage. She theorizes that romantic love is part of a reproductive strategy designed to keep couples together at least long enough to raise a child through infancy, at which point the child is able to run away from a lion/snake/hyena/elephant/cheetah/bear/coyote/large raccoon.

Obviously, there exist couples who have been together their

entire adult lives. I would guess that those people are either very lucky, very religious, or very, very good at conflict resolution. Many of those people were raised at a time when culture and divorce laws were much stricter, and a lot of those women never had the chance to become financially independent from their partners. Maybe a bunch of these people are very unhappy, maybe some of them are just genetically inclined to be chill and compromising, or maybe some of them made some bet with their homies that they'd stay married longer, who knows.

It's probably still POSSIBLE to make a careful and self-actualized choice and pick a lifelong partner who shares your values, who is a good hang, and who is emotionally capable of supporting you—a person who you could stay with throughout your entire life. As a lazy person, I would love to do this, because it seems easier than going through the whole dating process again once every three to ten years. But even if you pair up with an ideal partner, I think you'll likely find that the kind of love you feel for each other evolves throughout your life. And maybe you will also find that at some point you're going to at least experience, if not act on, romantic feelings for other people.

There are people who would argue that the solution is to have multiple romantic partners at the same time. I know that these people exist because they live in Brooklyn and they are always trying to get me to read *Sex at Dawn*. Personally, I've never been polyamorous—the most men I have ever been able to keep spinning at once was two, and even that fell apart after a couple weeks. Maybe it's because my iCal skills are not advanced enough, because I'm bad with names, or because I am brainwashed by society. Maybe

I just can't whip up enough interest! But alternatively structured relationships work for a lot of people—I know a ton of people who have happily spent time in open relationships (I live in Brooklyn). But I don't think nonmonogamous relationships magically solve all problems with love. Quite a few of my friends in open relationships have broken up with their primary partner. Some have broken up with all but one partner and become monogamous. And, of course, there's the danger that your multiple concurrent relationships are mimicking existing relationship and power structures that benefit men. As one friend told me, from experience: "You end up getting treated badly by six guys instead of one." Which isn't to say alternatively structured relationships are doomed to fail; it's to say basically all relationships are doomed to fail!

Given all this, should we even be bothering with love if there's virtually no chance that we're going to end up dying in the arms of our hot husband of 150 years?

Nothing in life lasts. Fruit rots, often before I even buy it. *Game of Thrones* is ending. Ozymandias turns into desert dust. Mary Shelley pushes her husband into a lake, or stabs him on a rowboat, or something? Channing Tatum and Jenna Dewan Tatum announce their separation. You die, Channing Tatum dies, everybody dies. The sun expands and burns up the Earth and after that all the energy in the universe devolves into entropy and all life and motion and heat in the universe expires forever. This is the kind of shit I liked to think about in college, when I was newly smart enough to know about "the heat death of the universe" but still too dumb to know there's no point in remembering the heat death of the universe once a month and spending the weekend bummed out.

All of this doesn't mean that it isn't enjoyable to eat cherries while watching *Game of Thrones*. Experiences are meaningful while they last—in fact, they're the whole point of it all. "The meaning of life is that it ends," said Kafka, who is now dead, proving everything.

You've got one dumb life on this planet to gobble up as much joy as you can, and a big part of that means finding people to fullheartedly love and to hopefully be loved by. Yeah, it's pretty much guaranteed that that love is going to end one way or another, but knowing that endings are natural means you don't have to feel shame when your love ends and when you find yourself loving multiple people over your lifetime. Breakups still feel shitty no matter what, but slightly less shitty when you don't take them as a personal indictment. And if you end up staying with one person, you can feel a lot saner when obstacles come up if you know going in that intense romantic love almost certainly doesn't last fifty straight years.

So as a poet once said, "Gather ye rosebuds while ye may, because you're young now and you're not going to be hot forever." You have to pursue love because love is great and fun and it's even more meaningful in each moment because of the fact that one day someone dies or you break up or your superhumanly strong wife, Mary Shelley, holds your head underwater because you didn't compliment her enough when she wrote *Frankenstein*. (I googled this and apparently Mary Shelley DID NOT murder her husband? This actually makes me like her a lot less?) But no matter how it ends, when it ends, be compassionate with yourself and each other. Breakups are natural; love is fake.

Rejection Is Good

There are a ton of stories about now-famous writers who, at the beginning of their careers, collected rejection letters. Stephen King tacked them up on his wall. Jessica Williams does the same in *The Incredible Jessica James*. Personally, I think this is over the top. I prefer to completely ignore my professional rejections or in VERY RARE cases send a polite email thanking them for my rejection before I move on with my life. This is partly because I don't like to dwell on things that don't work out and partly because there are so many better things to tack to your wall, such as pages from old One Direction calendars, your friends' art, photos of your aura, and pictures of the Rodham-Clinton family from Christmas 1994.

But it is true that in endeavors that involve vulnerability—writing, loving—you do have to expect a certain amount of rejection and you have to find a way to not let that rejection ruin you.

When I first started writing, for a college comedy YouTube show, my stuff was being read aloud in group pitch meetings where everything was anonymous, so when people didn't laugh at my jokes, I was at least protected from people knowing that I, specifically, was not funny. Even now, I send my pieces to editors or tweet out my little jokes and get rejected over the internet, at a distance. The only arena in which I would get rejected to my face is when I perform live, and that doesn't happen because, let's face it: I'm a comedic genius.

But romantic rejection is incredibly personal. It doesn't always happen right in your freaking face—I was first directly romantically rejected in the eighth grade, when I told my crush I had a crush on him over AIM and he told me he preferred being friends. I wish to God I had an exact record of this; Russia, if you're listening, I hope you're able to find my missing AIMs from middle school. Now that I'm thinking about it, a LOT of guys have rejected me over text and the internet. Maybe I should print THOSE out and turn them into wallpaper.

Either way, it's very easy to let romantic rejection ruin you, to take it as a referendum on your entire personality and physical appearance. I certainly took that eighth-grade rejection and reacted with a mixture of repression, self-consciousness about my still-malleable selfhood, and agony. I also then went and set my crush up with my best friend, because that is the kind of hurt I loved to luxuriate in back then.

I've since learned that, just as not everyone is going to love my rapid-fire jokes about period chunks, not every guy who is Hot to Me is going to be perfect or even slightly good for me. In fact, the large majority are not! Even when they seem to be because they are six foot three, have a British accent, and also like the song "Thunder Road" by Bruce Springsteen—I KNOW, that's THREE WHOLE THINGS, how could this not be the person I'm meant to spend the rest of my life with?!

As it turns out, the most important sign that someone is not right for you isn't how they feel about Harry Styles or whether they have glasses that make them look like a professor, but whether or not they're interested in you. If a guy isn't into me, we are not compatible, because I am very into me, specifically my boobs and knowledge of science and my jokes about period chunks. I absolutely have to be with a guy who is very jazzed about me because, otherwise, what's the point? Where's the fun? Contrary to ten billion years of books and movies, unrequited love is not romantic; it is very boring. We're all going to die in two to five years because [insert terrifying thing Trump is doing today], so why should I spend those years trying to convince some hot British guy that I'm worthwhile?

A friend of mine once told me that he hates Walt Whitman. He thinks Whitman is self-involved and boring. He can't even read a whole Whitman poem without being disgusted by Whitman's inability to see outside himself. This stressed me out. *Leaves of Grass* is foundational for me and for every artist I like. I have a Walt Whitman tattoo! I, a self-involved and boring nightmare, sometimes print out sections of "Song of Myself" and give them to my co-worker Jonah (a different person who does appreciate Whitman but isn't, perhaps, trying to read him during working hours)! It was incredibly important to me that I succeed in convincing my friend that Whitman is the greatest poet who ever lived, but even though I stayed up until three A.M. saying, "but . . . but . . . but . . . ," obviously this did not work. This doesn't lessen Whitman and it doesn't lessen my friend either, it just means that my friend has bad taste. I didn't put all this together until I made a move on this same guy and he politely told me he wasn't interested. I don't suck, and men who don't want to kiss me aren't necessarily cruel, they just have bad taste! They can't help it! Conversely, depending on how self-hating you're feeling at any specific moment, these men are not more special for seeing that you secretly ARE worthless. They're just normal men who don't want to be with you for whatever reason and who should, like all other men, probably carbon freeze themselves for twenty years to give us a break. Analyzing why these men don't love you is beneath you.

Rejection is very normal and is, in fact, good. It means that you are putting yourself out there, being brave. All I want in any aspect of my life is to be brave, like Indiana Jones or the kids in any kids' movie. And luckily, with practice, most rejection won't break your heart at all. At worst it will give you a bruise that you'll wake up with and be like, "How did I get this bruise?" And you won't remember. And you'll spend the day showing off your weird bruise that just showed up.

Ways to Break Up with Someone You Aren't Dating

- ◆ Never kiss them again and never ever mention that you have kissed them.
- ◆ Don't respond to a text that asks a direct question.
- ◆ Mention your new boyfriend/girlfriend to them.
- ◆ Slowly increase the amount of time you take to answer their texts until you are texting them once a month.
- ◆ Cancel three plans in a row.
- ◆ When they suggest a time for a date, say no and don't suggest an alternative time.
- ◆ Dramatically cut them out of your life even though you've only kissed once.

◆ Kick them out of your apartment mid-make out because they were paying too much attention to the One Direction documentary and not enough attention to you.
◆ Say "See you around."

Breakup Clichés

Writing is very hard. Saying things that are interesting and accurate and emotionally resonant—it is VERY DIFFICULT! Imagine me crying and checking Instagram five times while writing just this sentence; that is how difficult writing is.

Talking is usually easier because almost all the time no one really cares what you're saying. Maybe, like, they're listening to 40 percent of the information and words coming out of your mouth. But when you're breaking up with someone, people care. They are listening to 100 percent of the words coming out of your mouth, to take them home and break them up into sharp little pieces they'll examine and then stab into their brain just to relive the pain of it all.

So breakups run into a wall. You're trying to be kind, you're trying to save this person from hurt, and you're trying to be honest, but you're talking off the dome and you don't have the luxury of taking a frustrated nap while your subconscious "works out the syntax." You're looking at another person and maybe they have that LOOK on their FACE and you end up just saying a phrase that your neural networks have carved into your brain, because it's there in your mouth already and it basically captures the gist of what you were going for anyway. So you're like:

> *"It's not you! It's me!"*
> *"I'm sorry if I led you on!"*
> *"You deserve better than me!"*

Yes, that is what you meant to say, ish! However, it sounds like a lie to the other person, because they have already seen Hugh Grant saying these things in movies. And unlike Hugh Grant's fictional love interests, these are real and particular people experiencing genuine emotions.

I'm not against the idea of breakup clichés. As someone who spent thousands of dollars on improv classes and still came away kind of terrified of doing improv, and who sometimes finds herself saying "That sucks ass" forty times in a three-hour span, I know how hard it can be to speak extemporaneously. Doing that while also being both honest and kind about ending a relationship is maybe impossible. Human whim is capricious and at the end of the day we're all horny idiots. Maybe it's not NOBLE to end things with someone because it took you two months to decide if you thought they were hot and you ended up deciding they're not hot. But that doesn't make you a bad person. And so to a certain extent, "It's not you, it's me" is always gonna be true.

I do, however, have some problems with "Sorry if I led you on." This phrase is an abbreviation of a longer phrase with a very specific meaning, and it's not "Sorry I led you onto this ice floe, which is now drifting out to sea" or "Sorry if I led you on to believe that Tilda Swinton has two boyfriends, when, in fact, she does not." No, "Sorry if I led you on" is a shorter way of saying "Sorry if I led you on to believe that we were going to date/marry."

I never thought to think about this dumb li'l collection of words until a guy I was kissing recently ended things with me by using this phrase (via text, L O L). It made me so mad that I . . . continued running the errands I was doing, because I'm a busy career woman and I was out buying a good bra to wear to the Emmys. But: I was pissed!

This guy and I had only hooked up a few times, and he had told me repeatedly that he wasn't in an emotional place to date anyone. (A fascinating thing about me is that I'm only capable of meeting guys who can't emotionally handle dating right now.) The first time he told me this, I appreciated the heads-up. I was definitely bummed, because I liked him, but, like, he's his own dude and I get it. And since I like a clean narrative as much as the next girl, if this isn't leading to a point where I charm your entire family over a Jewish holiday I'd like to know that from the start, before I spend six months envisioning it before I fall asleep.

But every time after the first time that he told me he wasn't up to dating, it felt insulting. I had told him that I was cool with just hooking up, so it felt like he didn't believe me, that I, a GIRL, surely had to be merely TOLERATING his dick in order to TRAP him into a huge emotional and time commitment. Like he saw women as spiders who, once they had a juicy man in their web, rushed over to him and forced him to listen to how their day went. Or maybe he didn't see all women like this and it was something to do specifically with me. Either way, I would be like: "yeah" and "I know" and "I can look out for myself." Folks: it was not good. It's like the things we were saying had no relation to the things the other person was saying. I feel like he must have meant to say something else, but I have no idea what it was.

Another cliché men love to limply toss my way when they leave me is "You deserve better than me." But it's pretty easy to deal with this line: I just say, "Oh, it's okay, I'm an adult woman who can decide who is good enough for me, and I think you're fine." Then we get back to frenching. Voilà!

This doesn't work because people who say "You deserve better than me" are dirty liars. Everyone in the world secretly believes that they are, if not the BEST person in the world, then one of the best. "No!" you protest. "I'm a lazy piece of shit!" Maybe you truly think so, but in your most inner soul you also, incorrectly, believe that there is a realer, better version of you that only you know about because only you have access to your intentions and thoughts and to the whole universe inside you. Unfortunately, that's fake and the real you is the you everyone sees. To learn more about this philosophy, google "philosopher + there is no real inner you."

"You deserve better than me" is also total bullshit because no one in human history has ever sat down and made a pros and cons spreadsheet to see if they deserve their partner, and then ended things out of a sense of duty. What would even be on that spreadsheet? Height? Annual income? Personal best mile time? How much do they freak out when people ask what their favorite movie is? "Hot in Glasses"?

Actually, there are probably some weirdos among you who have made such a spreadsheet. Almost certainly Jeff Bezos has made one. Maybe, if I get very bored on some Saturday night, I will make one. But if you do end up deciding your partner is "better" than you (a fake concept!), you would definitely CONTINUE that relationship.

But men like to look down, blink a lot, and say in an extremely pained way that "You deserve better" because they're trying to act like you're both victims. He's the one breaking up with you, which is his choice and what he wants, but by saying it's for YOUR good he positions himself as deserving of sympathy. He can't even let you have your pain because THIS IS FOR YOU and HE'S BEING SELF-SACRIFICING. It's really fucked up and a little gaslight-y. Alanis Morissette screamed that it is not cool to give her a cross to bear and then deny it, and folks: she ain't wrong!

So I guess, in the scale of human events, people using clichés when they break up with you is not a huge deal. After all, if men don't say baffling things to me before running away, what else will I force my coworkers to listen to me rant about while they try to work?

But on the other hand: human relationships are always difficult to navigate, because we are all dinguses who can't decide if Jimmi Simpson is hot, let alone decide if we have the capacity to truly love another person more than ourselves. And it's even more difficult to navigate this stuff when you're a woman who is constantly getting bombarded by external stimuli designed to convince you that your body needs to look like something nonhuman-shaped in order to be hot, and that you're too obsessed with relationships but also you're worthless if you're not in one.

Given that I'm already machete-ing my way through that dense jungle of social conditioning, I wish men who are trying to break up with me would just speak honestly. I don't have TIME to sit and think about what this guy really meant when he said, "You deserve better than me." I have to figure out how to navigate the obvious and subtle ways in which I and others are oppressed! I have to think about things that are serious! I have to think, in minute detail, about the daily life of Karl Ove Knausgaard! How else will I ever be a respected writer?!

Lines I Would Prefer Men Use When Rejecting Me

- I don't want to kiss you, but I admire and am *inspired* by your courage in asking me to kiss you.
- I'm just at a point in my life right now where I NEED to have a giant, unkempt, gross beard, and I don't want to subject you to that.
- We don't live in the same city, we're never going to live in the same city, and even though I do like you, I think we should save two years of Amtrak fares.
- You're just too short. It hurts my back to kiss you. This isn't sustainable.
- Listen, you're a genius. You need a man who will dedicate his life to your art. And I hate reading.

◆ I know I said I couldn't date anyone right now, but I just meant that I couldn't date YOU, because you're so basically perfect that we'd immediately have to, like, get married. Anyway: I'm dating someone.

Ghosting

I don't need to define ghosting because everyone already knows what it is: a very rude way that scientists have invented for us to break up with one another.

Ghosting is founded on the belief that we are all so chill that when we are not compatible with another person, both parties will forget about each other at the exact same rate. We don't need to formally break up with each other because we mutually respond to texts slower and slower, until one day on our deathbed our great-great-grandchild Charbon scrolls through our phone and asks who "Josh TGI Fridays" is. And we, honestly, can no longer remember.

Of course, this never happens, or maybe happens to one lucky uncouple a year. If I had any faith in polling anymore, I would ask Nate Silver to look into it. Instead I will just confidently declare that one person in this situation is always, to some extent, agonizing. Because: How extremely rude is ghosting?! You, the ghoster, just stop responding to a person, the ghostee, as if they never deserved to have met you. Like they failed their audition to exist in your life and now they, a real-life person, have just vanished. I already suspect my phone, computer, and iMessage account are broken whenever my actual friends take longer than three hours to text me back. It's insane, in an age when we live through our phones, for a person to just stop texting you with no explanation!! There should be a *Twilight Zone* about this! Maybe there's already a *Black Mirror*, but again, I just cannot bring myself to watch that show: another reason men hate me!

It's supposed to be nicer, I guess, to spare a person the explanation of why you don't want to continue kissing them, instead skipping right to the point where you are already broken up. But, like I said in "Breakup Clichés," the world is already insane and predicated on a lot of bullshit, and, where I can get it, I like to know the truth. Even if the truth is "I personally don't think you're that hot" or "you scream too much on Monday mornings for me to deal with long-term."

Disappearing from a person's life, refusing to respond to texts and emails is called ghosting only when it's done in the beginning stages of an entanglement. But sometimes you have to do it to someone who is ingrained in your life and important to you. These are people who are never going to spontaneously forget you exist, no matter how many emails you don't respond to or how many social media sites you block each other on. Maybe you'll delete their number so your great-great-grandclone won't be able to ask you about them, but on your deathbed you'll summon your biographer just to clarify that you've always felt bad about the way things ended with Josh.

In these cases, disappearing from a person's life is a last resort. The decision to end a relationship is seldom easy to make. This is a person who has told you many times that you should be president, who introduced you to that goat who was trapped on a roof and respected only one man (google it), who legitimately wants to see you whenever you are free, who you have held while he cried. How do you weigh all that against the fact that they don't ever consider your emotions?

When you finally decide to end things, it's very possible that your mind is only 51 percent made up. And when you feel 49 percent sure that you still want to spend all your time with someone, it's very easy to be convinced that you should. God bless any person who wants to fight for their feelings, but when this has been going on for months, it's emotionally draining and pointless. You don't want to feel shitty all the time, even if it's only a very slight majority of the time—this is why, for example, I stopped watching *Frasier* straight through on Netflix. And if someone keeps trying to logic you out of your feelings, and you've already honestly explained them, sometimes you just have to stop responding to their emails.

But, as a little treat, keep one of their voice mails in case you're ever in the mood to be emotionally devastated.

Internet Stalking

There do exist reasons to internet stalk someone that aren't sad or creepy: maybe you just remembered this person for the first time in fifteen years, maybe you're going on a first date and want to make sure their Twitter handle isn't @LoveToDismemberWomen, maybe you just started watching *Riverdale* and you need to know where KJ Apa was born, his height, his age, what his accent sounds like, his natural hair color, and whether or not he reads books.

But pound for pound, when I google someone—especially when that someone is a guy I used to be into—it's usually because I'm in the mood to feel like someone is stabbing me in the stomach. It's for those moments when I'm like, *Hmm, I was just happily reading this Patti Smith book, but what if instead I look at pictures of this guy and the five hundred twenty-three-year-old girls he apparently hangs out with all the time now?*

Not all internet stalking is equal, of course. There's just googling someone, which, if all internet stalking is to some extent pervy, a simple google is like kissing in that it's really not pervy at all and you can do it on network sitcoms. Then there's scrolling through weeks of their tweets and Instagrams: it's normal, we all do it, but you gotta keep it to basic cable. And THEN there's the really fucked-up HBO-level shit, like looking at someone's tagged photos on Instagram or their likes on Twitter. You do it, but maybe you don't talk to your friends about the fact that you do it, and if someone did it on *Game of Thrones* it would spur a national conversation about whether it was bad for women.

We live in an age where people put a lot of information about themselves online. It's natural to be curious about people you've known or curious about people you may in the next month allow to be naked around you, and now it's just a lot easier to satiate that curiosity with a gigantic wave of LinkedIn endorsements and couchsurfing.com profiles. There's no reason to be ashamed of this thing that everyone does. I sometimes casually tell new romantic interests, "Oh, I saw that on your Facebook," in order to normalize even the lightest level of online research, although I've been trying to roll this strategy out since 2013 and it is still in beta.

It's also natural to want to make yourself feel bad in the days and weeks and months after severing a relationship with someone. It's easier than ever now, because we have such easy access to what these people are doing at any time. In the past maybe people stared at daguerreotypes and wondered which section of "Song of Myself" their ex was currently reading. When you've had the kind of breakup where only 51 percent of you wants to split, looking at photos of your person on Instagram can be a healthy way to manage the 49 percent of the time that you want to get back together with them. You can feel like you're there with them at their birthday party as they receive a "birthday cuck" badge, without having to prolong your breakup by five hundred years. Thus you save much sadness for both of you and avoid getting to a point where you text them "I miss you" and they text back "hahahahahahahaha."

I am a big, huge fan of feeling and experiencing your emotions. I love to cry and I love to text people about the fact I'm crying. I love to shriek so much I laugh and then laugh so hard I sob, at work, in other people's offices! But when making the decision to no longer include in your life someone you used to care about, especially when you still feel a lot of love for that person, I think it's only hurtful and inconsiderate to equivocate. So instead I deal with that by talking to friends and writing and performing immersion therapy on myself, looking at photos of them with their young hot New Versions of Me enough until it doesn't hurt anymore.

What I Am Hoping Comes Up When I Internet Stalk People

New crushes: a good Twitter. Ideally I would love to date some man, any man, who isn't in the New York comedy scene. Until then, I at least want my crushes' Twitters to be funny.

Old crushes: wedding Web site. The platonic ideal of googling your high school crush is a huge life divergence. He's getting married to a long-distance runner named Biscayne and I write tweets about how I am bad at dating and all men hate me.

Exes: they moved far away. I can stop imagining running into them on the subway and instead imagine them terrorizing all the women of Omaha.

New crushes: astrological sign. There's nothing worse than going on multiple dates with a guy before finding out he's a Virgo.

Old crushes: photo of him senior year of high school when he had pink hair and I had such a crush on him that I told my mom I wanted to dye my hair pink and she said she would kick me out

of the house. Just ONE photo! What the hell happened to his Xanga?!

New crushes: video of them talking. It's almost like getting to hang out with them.

New crushes: video of them singing. Even better.

New crushes: video of them singing while playing an instrument. Jesus Christ.

Old crushes: they committed a murder. It's very sad BUT: it's also very interesting.

New crushes: news article about how he fell into a large manhole (he's fine) or about his upcoming wilderness science expedition. Only applies if he is currently not answering my texts.

Exes: they wrote a book. Reading an ex's book is, like, extremely advanced internet stalking.

New crushes, old crushes, exes, celebs: at least one objectively hot photo I can show my friends to prove this guy is hot. This one is tragically difficult to find. HOT MEN NEED TO BE MORE ACTIVE ON INSTAGRAM.

Pop Culture Anniversaries

As someone who has somewhat briefly and very intensely become emotionally involved with a string of men, as opposed to spent twenty years married to the same guy and then gotten divorced, I don't relate to the trope of "It's Christmas and . . . [sobs] . . . I'm ALONE!" There's a whole genre of "I'm alone on an important holiday" sadness: I'm alone on Thanksgiving, I'm alone on New Year's, it's Sukkot and I'm alone, why, God, why?? Probably I don't care about this because I still spend holidays with my family. I'm like, "It's Christmas and . . . [sobs] . . . my brother stuffed a rotting banana in my Doc Marten and then put it on top of the highest cabinet."

The thing that, for me, triggers a realization that my life is hollow without [insert man] is the release of a new movie in a franchise or a season in a show that I had watched with some dude. In our happiest times, he would come over late at night and we would watch *The Leftovers*. It was so bleak, but, Carrie Coon! And wow, Justin Theroux is very hot and good at acting and how wild is it that he wrote *Tropic Thunder*?! And the first season was kind of boring but if you just invested ten hours of your sacred life, the second season was so good! But when a prestige drama has only ten episodes per season there's a lottttt of time between seasons to, like, cut someone entirely out of your life. And then all of a sudden *The Leftovers* is back and you have no one to talk about it with anymore and you can't figure out if you even care about this show or if you just like cuddling on a weeknight and also YOU MISS HIM SO MUCH.

"Find someone else to talk to about *The Leftovers*," says you, completely misunderstanding the entire cultural moment. Peak TV has given us a lot of gifts, but it has also given us way too many options. "TV is triage," says *New Yorker* TV critic Emily Nussbaum, and while you may assume that everyone you know must watch *The Leftovers*, that's the same type of thinking that made you so sure Hillary was going to win. Apparently millions of people watch *The Big Bang Theory* and voted for Trump and you don't know a single one of them.

It's also VERY HARD to profile who might watch *The Leftovers*. And unlike "being over six feet tall" or "being very famous," there's no dating app to help you single these people out. (Can you believe there's a dating app for being over six feet tall?!)

Listen, I have life experiences. I go on road trips with my friends from growing up. I . . . go to work. But a lot of my time is spent writing, being sneezed on by a tall person on the subway, or watching TV. So when suddenly I don't have anyone to talk to about my theories or show crushes it makes a person's absence very obvious in a way it rarely is otherwise.

It's not just *The Leftovers*, by the way. Some other art that reminds me that I will die alone: the *Fast and the Furious* movie franchise, *Wet Hot American Summer*, Martin McDonagh films, the fact that Martin McDonagh is hot. Martin McDonagh: he is problematic for sure. He is also hot!

If you are cool and single and want to talk to me about any of these, please feel free to find me on the dating app Twitter.

Getting Back Together

One of the tenets of the Crone Collective, an art collective/coven/
party-hosting organization I co-run, is "People always do exactly
what they want to do." Listen: this is the most genius thing you
have ever heard. It could be an entire philosophy book unto itself.
People ALWAYS DO WHAT THEY WANT TO DO. I could cite
some white male philosophers to convince you of this or you could
just think about it for two seconds and realize that, yes, people always do what they want. (It's especially true of men, who aren't
taught to be self-sacrificing and to submit to a social structure that
oppresses them.)

Since learning this true idea from my co-crone-in-chief Madelyn Freed, I have usually meditated on it when I worry that I have
trapped someone into hanging out with me even though that person hates me and would rather be anywhere else in the world, even,
like, watching CNN on a twenty-four-hour loop while very hungry
but not sure if they want to eat something sweet or salty. In those
moments I tell myself: everyone always does what they want
to do, and this person is hanging out with me because they want to.

Unfortunately, people are also doing exactly what they want
when they break up with you. Men break up with me because they
want to break up with me. I, a woman with way too much confidence gained from listening to Spice Girls and reading Caitlin
Moran, am able to accept this for about a week before I become convinced that the man in question made a mistake. I have literally
said the phrase "I'm pretty sure he didn't know what he wanted,

so I'm gonna give him another chance." As in I, the person who got dumped, am going to give another chance to the person who dumped me. In my mind I'm giving them a chance to pretend like they never broke up with me, but in reality I'm giving them a chance to break up with me again.

I guess I'm able to convince myself that people "made a mistake" because I have a very broad interpretation of what are considered "flirty vibes." And to be completely fair to myself, this doesn't *not* work. You give people who used to like to kiss you a chance to kiss you again and often they will do it. Maybe they're just looking for someone to kiss, or maybe they're still in that phase of ending something where a healthy percentage of the time they'd rather still be kissing you. But I've found that eventually it becomes clear that they broke up with you because they wanted to, and it wasn't a mistake, and by giving them another chance you're just causing pain for yourself and for everyone who has to deal with the two of you.

And also: life is short. I'm for sure going to die young from too many years of hubris about being vegan and never eating protein, or from thermonuclear war after some dumb-ass three A.M. tweet, or from my roof falling in on me when my twenty-eight-year-old blond Edgar Allan Poe–looking neighbor has a party that is Too Cool. So there really is not any time available to be in a relationship with someone who isn't jazzed to be in it. And I KNOW, you're like, "NO ONE wants to kiss me and I will kiss ANYONE who is willing even if they are EXTREMELY LUKEWARM ABOUT IT." I have been there! I get that people make it seem as if the choice is between kissing someone who is very stoked about kissing you or kissing someone who doesn't really want to kiss you (a very obvious choice), when it's often between kissing someone who is meh on the whole situation or not kissing anyone at all.

I understand the impulse to kiss someone who isn't very into you. But get those kisses out of your system and then go do something better with your time. Because the real choice is between kissing someone who is meh about you or reading a book or going to the Poconos, sitting in a twenty-five-foot-tall rocking chair, and thinking: Wow. People used to be so much taller.

Love Amnesia

Have you ever found old flirty texts or, god forbid, love letters, and just felt absolute curiosity that you ever felt that way about that person? That's love amnesia, when you've moved on so totally that you can no longer summon even wisps of how you used to love someone.

I encounter this feeling most frequently when I stumble upon long emails I sent to crushes, giving them (solicited) notes on their writing. There was a time in my life where I would write PARAGRAPHS, full sentences complete with punctuation and capital letters where necessary, to men, with thought-out ways for them to improve their bad art. Now that I'm a five-hundred-year-old feminist who is very busy, I don't do this anymore. For one, I don't want to use whatever small amount of power I've amassed in the comedy world to help A MAN. Men are already doing fine. So now, even when the men asking me for notes are very cute, even if I'm kissing them, I just say, "I would cut down the beginning and take out any bits that aren't jokes." It turns out this advice is correct 100 percent of the time. One day, probably, my prince will come, and instead of him kissing me and waking me from an enchanted slumber, I will know he is The One because he will ask me for notes and I will be psychically capable of giving them.

But for now, it is very strange to read these emails from a version of me who I know at the time burned with an emotion I can no longer remember feeling. In a way it's nice to know that I used to feel a yearning or a pain that I no longer feel. In another way, it makes me feel very old and dead inside. Like: Oh my god, I used to be capable of such emotion! I used to be so free and giving with my love and admiration and critical reading powers in a way I may never be again! I think about how fervently I crushed on one boy throughout high school and know I will never be so obsessed with a dude ever again, unless I start taking some form of birth control that messes with my hormones in a probably lethal way.

Feeling nothing is better than feeling like hell every time you encounter an old voice mail from a guy that he left you while you were peeing, where he says he wants you to stuff him like an old grizzly bear when he dies and put him in your living room to scare your parents. It's much better than feeling searing anger and hurt whenever you think about them. Between feeling lingering bitterness and feeling shock at my lack of any emotions at all, I'd rather feel nothing.

Oh, Haha, We Used to Kiss

The goal that everyone claims to aspire to is being friends with their exes. But, like, how? Friendship—mutual respect and good feeling and lack of sexual tension—is a very complicated aioli to whisk up when you're starting at a place of anger or hurt on at least one side, but also maybe a lot of residual love and boners for one another. Is it possible to become such normal friends with an ex that you end up telling other friends who had no clue: "Oh, haha, yeah, we used to kiss, a million years ago"?

"Exes" is a strong word for me to use and maybe not technically warranted: when I say "ex," I'm talking about men who I kissed for a period of time between, like, once and for a couple months. Maybe we were *emotionally* involved for longer than that, but also we were never officially dating, so can we be officially exes? It's just easier than launching into a thirty-minute explanation before making an offhand, boring comment about someone I kissed twice in 2015. That being said! I think I'm a pretty good person to have had made out with. (I recently said this to someone who told me he couldn't make out with me because we are "too close to too many of the same people and what if it went wrong?" It did not convince him!) But I think my track record is pretty good at being normal friends with people I used to kiss.

Although I've gleaned from men that I project some sort of slash-and-burn, General-Sherman-marching-to-the-ocean vibe when it comes to exes—one man told me that he didn't want to be "one of the men you don't talk to anymore"—I've really only cut off communication with two exes. One was deliberately and clearly, and one was kind of by default after he ghosted me, moved across the country, and then requested to connect with me on LinkedIn. I'm truly not even sure how this happened, as I don't think I have a LinkedIn? Some dudes were only tenuously in my life before we kissed and are only tenuously in my life now that we don't. A couple are in that comfortable love amnesia territory, where it's wild to me that I ever salivated and worried over them and now feel generally fondly toward them. And a few of these men were basically nothing to me before we kissed and are now some of my closest male friends.

I am *very* thankful to have these men in my life and, as divorced parents often say about their kid [looks wistfully into a cloud for five seconds], "I don't regret any of it because I got Michael out of it." But that doesn't mean that the way I got from kissing to friendship was healthy! Mainly it happened because we kissed a couple times and then I spent an extremely absurd amount of time—like, almost a year in some cases?—in denial that we had really kissed for the *last* time. You, smart, well-adjusted: "How could you spend that long in denial that someone wasn't into you?" Well, I thought maybe they *wanted* to kiss me, but I was too busy to hang out (I'm writing all the time, I have a lot of shows, I'm out of town a solid 50 percent of weekends) or they were too busy to hang out (I'm attracted to busy people: I'm a female Sagittarius and I need to be in a power couple). These guys and I *did* hang out once or twice a month, maybe, and even though they never kissed me I always found a way to rationalize it. (He HAD to get into an Uber to take him across Brooklyn because he was very tired, and he couldn't kiss me before he left in case one of his exes saw from down the block!) (Now in retrospect I've convinced myself again!) Plus: sometimes you *do* start kissing someone again after a long break. It has happened to me maybe . . . thrice. Which is all to say that by the time I truly accepted it into my heart that these guys did not ever in their long lives want to kiss me again, I had unknowingly laid a lot of hangout foundation for what had already, surprisingly, become a pretty solid friendship.

The idea that being friends with exes is a great and noble goal is not as universally accepted as I assumed. "I don't think it necessarily is," says my friend Paul Gale. "Sometimes it's people hanging on to each other for longer than they should." Paul makes a very good and smart point. In most cases for *me*, personally, I don't think the men were holding on to me for longer than they should have. When it was, it seemed to correlate to things *explicitly* ending. I was told that romance was off the table, then the guy kept wanting to hang out while projecting low but still radioactive levels of sexual vibes. (My sexual vibes Geiger counter is pretty much *always* picking up trace vibes, but I'm talking about the cases when it's pretty obviously going *ding ding ding.*) (In my opinion, Geiger counters make a "ding ding" noise.) The problem I had with those flirty vibes from men who said they didn't want to kiss me wasn't that they were flirting—it was that I was being told that the vibes I was picking up on weren't actually happening. (They were. Who cares.)

I am going to go ahead and say that all of this is worth it! Really, genuinely being friends with someone you used to kiss is a blast. Part of the reason I wanted to kiss them in the first place is that they are cool people! Just because they don't want to smooch me anymore doesn't mean they aren't cool, still. Experiencing these men without that sexual element is really nice. It's fun and hilarious to learn about them as actual human people, as opposed to love interests whose faults you ignore for as long as possible. It's a relief to hang out with them without trying to appear hot and interesting! My friend Zach Zimmerman says that gay best friends get sex out of the way early. "Refreshing a straight pair can too!" Sometimes it's weird for me, when I'm, like, scheming to sleep with their friends, but I think that's just because I always assume people are feeling more emotions than they are. (Maybe this would be solved if I listened to podcasts during my commute instead of spending an hour and a half a day listening to Joni Mitchell and imagining all the emotions everyone I know is [not] feeling.) If you're able to get to a point where you feel platonically about someone—even if you sometimes, like I do, get random LSD flashbacks of "flirty vibes"—I highly recommend.

How to Get the Perfect Revenge Body

Step one: Have a body.
Step two: Use it to stab your ex.

7 BEING SINGLE

Full Tree

Despite my best efforts to never allow random men to talk to me, something a random man said to my family and me has become a defining phrase of my life. When I was young, my mom rounded up my family to take us somewhere to adopt a cat. We ended up falling in love with a pair of cats, a brother and sister that I named Kimi and Chuckie after the redheaded Rugrat and his adopted Parisian (??) sister. As we were adopting them, some rando saw what we were doing and, being the white man that he was, felt entitled to comment on it. "It's good that you're taking both of them," he said. "Alone, they could never become a full tree." It was an honestly ludicrous thing to say about two cats, but the phrase "full tree" has been part of my family vernacular since. We use it to mean a self-actualized person, someone complete in themselves and operating at their maximum capacity. I now know that I, as a single woman, am a full tree.

Getting to experience romantic love is definitely a dope-as-hell part of existing, but it's by no means a necessary prerequisite to being a full tree. Frida Kahlo said, "It's not love, or tenderness, or affection, it's life itself"'; some rando said, "You're nobody till somebody loves you." (Wikipedia says that rando is "Russ Morgan, Larry Stock, and James Cavanaugh" back in the year 1944.) They were all wrong. Or maybe Frida was partly right: love is a great and exciting thing to happen in the life of a tree, and excitement about ANYTHING is basically the point of life itself. But falling in love doesn't validate you as a full tree and it doesn't mean *Oh my god, now I *finally know* what it is to be a tree!* It's easy to feel like love IS life when (a) you're a woman who is told she NEEDS to find a man to be complete—because it serves the nefarious purposes of patriarchy, and (b) you're a human in an increasingly secular age where you are less likely to draw your sense of self from religion.

Plus, anyone who is interested in romantically loving another tree is going to spend periods alone, pissed at your partner, pissed at all of your seven partners. The powerful play goes on, you may contribute a verse, and you can't hang your worth on whether or not you die in your hot husband's arms.

I do, sometimes, wonder: Could I be *more happy,* a *fuller* tree, if I had a boyfriend? It's not a very empowered question, and it's definitely not a helpful thought in any way, but it's something that I have felt and wondered often, despite those things. (Though it works the other way as well: my current mind-set is closer to "I'm stressed, but I bet I could be EVEN MORE STRESSED if I had a boyfriend!") The idea is similar to women who say they never knew how much love they could feel until they gave birth and felt their capacity for love expand an insane amount. I have suspected the same could happen to my capacity for happiness, given the right partner. Or it's like: they say money doesn't make you happy, but studies have proven that's only true after you have a certain amount of money to live comfortably. Is there a certain amount of romantic love, some threshold, you have to meet to be baseline happy? Is it a boyfriend? A husband? Two husbands?

Maybe two husbands will make you happier for a bit, but you, and I, and every other person are already hovering around our baseline level of happiness (this is called the "happiness set point" and has been written about by psychologists since the 1970s). And so: you, right now, are a full tree. You don't need to be in love to count as a human. Look—you already ARE a human, existing! If anything is special in the world it's you, a bunch of insane neurons floating around in a body, getting to spend hopefully no less than seventy and no more than ninety years swimming and listening to One Direction and laughing with your family and begging your dad to stop explaining improv to you on the phone. For those years and, if Elon Musk has his maniacal way, many more thousands of years as a disembodied consciousness in the cloud, you start out as a full tree and just explore what kind of tree you are. When you figure it out, you get to focus on being the best version of that kind of tree!

Prose Before Bros

"Prose before bros" is a phrase that I was led to believe was created by one of my former crushes, but came to find out exists on thousands of shirts, mugs, and tote bags that you can buy at www dot the internet dot com. It describes the prioritization of writing over actual kissing. As in, I am single because I do not have time to date, because I am always inside writing about how I am single.

Historically, it has been much easier for a man to have both a serious writing career and a serious romantic partner, because his partner would do all the domestic work of supporting them both. You've got your Véra Nabokov, your Nora "James Joyce's Wife" Barnacle, your every woman Gustave Flaubert ever met. Basically any random schmuck could decide he wanted to be a writer, and he didn't have to worry about how he'd keep the house clean and the food cooked and the children supervised. He wouldn't even have to type up the pages! History is riddled with stories of genius men walking around dictating as their wives and daughters wrote or typed what he said. This is because, as I often say and as is legally provable, all men are illiterate.

For women, deciding to prioritize writing was a much more difficult and much more radical thing to do. They would have to never marry (Dickinson, Austen) or have an exceptionally woke husband (Virginia Woolf). And obviously there were many more obstacles to overcome for any woman who wasn't rich and white. But it's easier now, and getting easier despite the best efforts of Mike and Karen ("Mother") Pence.

Roger Ebert describes this prioritization of creative work over love extremely well in his review of *Broadcast News*, which I was alerted to by an excellent piece by Haley Mlotek in *The Ringer*. Ebert says that the movie is "about three people who toy with the idea of love, but are obsessed by the idea of making television," and that James L. Brooks is one of the only directors who "knows that some people have higher priorities than love, and deeper fears." Maybe I'm really staying inside instead of accepting an offer to see Destroyer in concert because I love the control I have in my writing, which I don't get in actual dating. But I hope I am staying inside because I have higher priorities than love! And deeper fears (the heat death of the universe)!

Is my "Prose before bros" philosophy costing me boyfriends? Well, I don't really think I'm missing out on boyfriends because of the time constraints. I'm not exactly referring dozens of hot men to my personal assistant to try to squeeze onto my schedule. Maybe my "obsessed by the idea of making television" vibe is turning them off—it's very possible that my aura alerts men that my pure heart is willed toward writing structural jokes and not being a fun, hot hang whenever.

But I know for sure that the fact that I am a woman who writes about love is costing me boyfriends. A guy I hooked up with a couple times has straight-up told me on multiple occasions that the writing I do is intimidating, and he can see why men would hesitate to date me (he was using the term "men" to mean "me, specifically, sorry"). Although on the other hand, one guy told me I should go even harder on men in my book than I was intending to. I assumed he didn't realize that *he* was in the book, but when I warned him, he wrote out and signed a hasty contract promising not to be mad "re: any book things." An extremely bold flirt!

At the end of the day, who cares. I mean, probably a lot of things are costing me boyfriends, and at least writing is one that I both value and enjoy. As Lady Gaga said, "Some women choose to follow men, and some women choose to follow their dreams. If you're wondering which way to go, remember that your career will never wake up and tell you that it doesn't love you anymore."

Comfort

Being single is comfortable. When I'm single I don't have to wear makeup, I don't have to do my hair, and when it's March and everyone else is out wearing hot-girl dresses and freezing their asses off, I can just wear a sweater and my extremely unflattering Hillary (RIP) sweatpants: fine, whatever.

I've recently learned that you can do all those things when you have a partner, too, especially once you've been seeing each other for a while and have come to terms with the fact that they realize you are a normal human. It feels like a huge relationship step to show a man my natural hair texture, but also: most men I kiss already knew what I looked like before I developed a crush and decided I needed to look nice when I saw them! I was reminded of this when I recently brought a new crush up to my apartment for the first time. I was in a low-cut red dress, hair curled with a straightener, mascara on, and feeling pretty good about myself until he walked over to my closet, pointed to my flannels, and said, "This is the area you draw from most." *HOW DID HE KNOW!?!?!* I thought, before remembering I'd known him for a solid two years before deciding he was hot.

More than the physical comfort of elastic-waist pants and being able to rub your eyes without looking like a raccoon, the comfort of being single is more about being able to do whatever you want, whenever you want, without having to consider anybody else's schedule or desires. You can eat whenever you want without considering if your partner is going to want to eat later; you don't have to keep a certain night open because it's the only night they have off work; if you decide at the last minute that you'd rather not travel an hour by two trains to get to a party, you have no obligation to go just because you're sleeping with the host!

That kind of comfort, too, can be achieved regardless of relationship status. You just gotta set some boundaries and say, "I need a little bit of time to take care of myself and do whatever the helk I want." (Is this "self-care"? I guess, probably, it is? But I worry about overusing that term, especially as a white woman. When Audre Lorde, a queer black woman, said, "Caring for myself is not self-indulgence, it is self-preservation, and that is an act of political warfare," I don't think she was talking about sticking a sixty-six-dollar jade egg up your vagina.) But if you want a night alone, you can literally just tell your boo to please get lost for the evening. And a little bit goes a long way! During the years I lived with roommates, I thought my introversion was bottomless, that I would never have enough alone time to feel fully recharged. Then I lived alone for like thirty hours. Now I spend all my time whispering, "I miss my friends."

When You Least Expect It

Everyone says you'll find love when you least expect it. Like, legitimately, actual people in my real life have said these exact words to my face since I was in high school. I'd be like, "Uh . . . okay, I'm really just focusing on getting into a good college!" (An obvious lie; I was splitting my focus between getting into a good college and getting my crush to ask me out.) (Insane that it's easier to get into Harvard than it is to get A*** P******* to fall in love with you.)

But "you'll find love when you least expect it"—what does that even mean?! It's a very messed-up thing to say to someone! It's a phrase that pretty much exists only to police women into chilling out, even though we're socialized to always be looking for a man. It tells women not to pay attention to people who are into you, and not to pursue people who you're into. Which is a pretty bad way to find love. Like: take the argument to its logical conclusion. I least expect to find love while trapped in a pitch-black cave that I have explored on a photo exhibition from *National Geographic*. And honestly: I doubt there are any hot, emotionally available men also trapped in that cave! "You'll find love when you least expect it" is basically a patriarchal double bind for women along the lines of the idea that "What Makes You Beautiful" is in fact being blind to your own beauty. (Though I will admit, after seeing Harry Styles perform that song in a folksy style in concert, my thoughts on the problematic nature of that song are *evolving.*)

The only way this statement makes sense is if everyone, *somehow*, finds love—if finding love is a given element of every single person's life on the planet. In that case, sure, maybe it will happen to you when you're not looking out for it. When I was a little girl, too young to date, I assumed that of course I would end up in love within a couple years: that's what I had been taught by every piece of media I had ever consumed (mostly Disney princess movies and *You've Got Mail* five hundred thousand times in a row). When I got to high school I thought the same, even as my friends started dating and I remained alone. After all, I was basically having an emotional affair with the captain of the football team—it wasn't my fault that he was also dating a conventionally hot field hockey player! I was love-adjacent; it seemed very possible that if I just stopped hoping and paying attention, I'd stumble into a tenable romantic situation.

But as high school and then college went by and I miraculously managed to escape love the entire time, I really and genuinely to my bones stopped expecting love. Because it turns out that if you spend all your time either doing homework or producing a comedy show, never putting yourself in situations where people expect to find romantic partners (parties, bars) and never considering yourself hot, it's very easy to not meet people, or at least not meet people who think to consider you a dating prospect. AND YET! Even though! I spent four years "least expecting" to find love . . . I STILL DIDN'T FIND IT!

I'm living now through a period of cognitive dissonance: I don't expect love to just fall into my lap because I don't expect *anything* to just fall into my lap, other than maybe gross AC water or pigeon poop, and honestly both of those things are more likely to fall directly onto my recently blow-dried hair. On the other hand,

I DO expect to find love, because, let's face it: I'm hot and funny! I just expect that I'll have to, like, make an effort. I've realized the "when you least expect it" adage may have been true back in the day when people got married very young; when you're a teen, the government mandates that you leave your house and go to a building where you interact with other teens for 180 days of the year. But as a single adult woman—one of an increasing number of them—I know I'll only find love if I open myself up emotionally and pursue men in person or at least on my phone. So don't say, "You'll find love when you least expect it" to anyone, probably, but especially not to single women. To us, it just means "Be less desperate."

MAKING ART

Making Art About Your Relationships

Women writing about their relationships are pathologized, punished, and diminished in a truly stunning number of ways. It's almost like we live in a patriarchal society where every aspect of culture is designed to take away women's power!

I want to talk a little bit about Taylor Swift, although she has become what the kids (thirty-five-year-olds on the internet) call "a problematic fave." She's a conventionally hot white woman from a very privileged background who spent pretty much her entire pre-*Reputation* career playing the victim. Which I get! People who are rich and hot and white are allowed to be sad and victimized in their personal life. Just because you're privileged doesn't mean your life is perfect, as many white men have shouted at me. But Taylor playing the victim became grating when she used that stance to be intentionally blind to structural racism (see: her response to Nicki

Minaj's critique of the VMAs only nominating videos that celebrate "women with very slim bodies"). The look is not great! Maybe spend a couple hours on Tumblr, Taylor! Maybe read some bell hooks!

Lately I'm trying to have more empathy for her, because we all do very dumb shit in our lives and the world is changing very fast and it can be hard to see how we need to change as well. And while I physically couldn't listen to her music for a very long time after she failed to use her vast platform to denounce Donald Trump, forcing me to add her to my "People Responsible for the Results of the 2016 Election" spreadsheet (also on there: Vladimir Putin, James Comey, Dean Baquet, Donald Trump)—she DID recently, finally, urge her fans to vote, and to vote for Democrats. SO: I have at times been extremely frustrated with Taylor Swift AND ALSO I have been very inspired by her emotional specificity and vulnerability and also by her handling of the backlash she has gotten for those things.

In case you somehow evaded Taylor Swift's mandatory Leave No Child Unaware of Who Taylor Swift Is ten-year press initiative, Taylor has spent her career making commercially and (generally) critically successful art about her experiences as a young woman attracted to men. This irked many people in such a way that their hair caught on fire and the only cure was intense media focus on Taylor's love life, calling her boy crazy and needy and psycho. In a profile of Taylor for a 2013 *Vanity Fair* cover story, Nancy Jo Sales asked Taylor if she was boy crazy (specifically after Taylor had just said that she wasn't boy crazy and was in fact work crazy). Taylor responded, "For a female to write about her feelings, and then be portrayed as some clingy, insane, desperate girlfriend in need of making you marry her and have kids with her, I think that's taking something that potentially should be celebrated—a woman writing about her feelings in a confessional way—that's taking it and turning it and twisting it into something that frankly is a little sexist."

As much as Taylor has since 2013 arguably commodified feminism for her personal gain and no one else's, that statement strikes me as so true. That statement changed my life!

Then there are the women like Joyce Maynard who are called narcissists and opportunists for writing about their own lives. According to this line of thinking, the fact that J. D. Salinger was beloved and notoriously private means that he owned what happened between him and Joyce Maynard more than she did. This, despite the fact that what happened between them was he (one of the country's most famous authors, then in his fifties) coerced an eighteen-year-old aspiring writer to abandon her life and enter into a sexual relationship with him at his New Hampshire house. Which, as you will immediately realize or currently are on a five-to-ten-year journey to realizing, is extremely fucked up!! That power differential is NOT OKAY! It may be technically legal, but it is very, very gross. Salinger's obsession with privacy seems a lot less quirky when you learn that he had a lifelong pattern of inappropriate emotional and sexual attachments to teen girls. "For Esmé—with Love and Squalor" is not as cute when you realize Salinger probably wanted to fuck Esmé! Sylvia Plath was also called a narcissist throughout her life. A guy once referred to my art as narcissistic, as a flirt. The flirt was not well received!

Anyways—the point of this is—women own the things that

happen to them, even if these things happened between them and much more powerful or well-known men. Writing about these things does not make women narcissists.

And THEN there are the people who get their undies in a bundle because they have a strong feeling that women who write about their relationships are giving too much of themselves away. This concern strikes me as super faux because I have never heard of men worrying that Jack Kerouac gave too much of himself away in the five hundred thousand novels he wrote about himself and his friends. Men are just like, "Yes, this is good, every eighteen-year-old should read this to learn how to go on pretty boring road trips and treat women like shit." Same goes for Karl Ove Knausgaard and the five hundred thousand novels he wrote about himself and . . . his breakfast cereal? Yet, in the Joni Mitchell biography *Reckless Daughter*, David Yaffe writes about how Kris Kristofferson once advised Joni to put less of herself in her art. (Wild that there was ever a time that any human being felt they had the right to give advice to Joni Mitchell. Wilder that I'm sure there are still many men who would feel very comfortable doing this!) Joni said of her contemporaries: "The vulnerability freaked them out."

The flip side of all of this "YOU ARE TRULY CRAZY AND RUINING YOUR LIFE WITH THIS KIND OF WRITING" moral panic is when art that women make about their relationships is called "relatable." "Relatable" is a very sexist word that men use to describe women's writing in order to diminish it. It says that when women write about experiences that resonate with people, it's a cheap, small thrill devoid of literary merit and based solely on recognition. Like when a comedian makes a joke about Pringles and people laugh just because they're like, "I've eaten Pringles, too!" But when men write about experiences that resonate with people, it's fulfilling David Foster Wallace's maxim that "fiction's about what it is to be a fucking human being."

Basically, women writing about their relationships are either seen as pathological (as if every person of every gender identity isn't driven pathologically insane by not only love but also day-to-day life) OR they are seen as frivolous (and not just because they're writing about love and not the Napoleonic Wars! When men write about love and relationships other men are like [starts clapping, slowly stands up and claps louder while *almost* crying], "That was so brave"). These dismissals are one way that society keeps women from speaking about the power structures that allow men to oppress women in an intimate setting.

And the real kicker is: how the HELK are women supposed to create brilliant art *without* tapping into their personal experiences? Art is better when it is specific! It's funnier: the classic example that I learned in five hundred different improv classes is saying "car" is less funny than saying "Toyota Yaris." I thought that example was kind of weak until two members of my sketch team wrote a bit about businessmen who see and become obsessed with a fancy car on the street. The sketch was basically eight minutes of them saying "Mazda Miata"; it killed.

Personal experience gives art a sense of emotional stakes. See: Nora Ephron's *Heartburn*. It's a movie (first a book, but I'm talking about the movie) about a woman whose journalist husband cheated on her, made by a woman whose journalist husband cheated on her. That raw feeling really elevates the film in a way that is only topped by a scene where Meryl Streep lounges on a couch in an evening dress, eating pizza. As the kids say: Iconic! A mood! Mom! TFW!

It's not just "relatable" women who believe that personal stakes make for better art. Take it from noted white dude who went to Princeton F. Scott Fitzgerald. In a letter to aspiring writer Frances Turnbull, included in *F. Scott Fitzgerald: A Life in Letters*, he writes: "I'm afraid that the price for doing professional work is a good deal higher than you are prepared to pay at the present. You've got to sell your heart, your strongest reactions, not the little minor things that only touch you lightly, the little experiences that you might tell at dinner."

So according to F. Scott Fitzgerald, if this woman doesn't write about her own experiences and her own emotions, she will never make great art. And, according to all of society, if she *does* write about those things, she's being crazy or selfish or "relatable." The extremely bonkers thing about this advice is that "Scott" or "F." or "Fran" or whatever people called him was very often stealing the emotions and experiences of his much more interesting and cool wife, Zelda! And when she tried to reclaim those things and write about them herself, Scott called her crazy and threw her in a mental institution. WHERE SHE DIED IN A FIRE. Please go read *Heroines* by Kate Zambreno to learn about this. Do not read another book by a man until you do!

I will say that I hate when people make "relationship" art that they don't actually care about, like people who respond to guys on Tinder using only *Mean Girls* quotes, so that they can write an article about it. Maybe these women are working through something important to them and intentionally seeming flippant about it. Maybe they are trying to assert some control over this marketplace they feel forced into, and this is their truth. But my truth is that this kind of thing is extremely annoying to me! It's the worst of both worlds. It feels like these interactions have no stakes, and if they have no stakes for you, why write about them?! Go live your life, rent a kayak, go to an art gallery or something. And the dudes on the other side of those conversations, structurally powerful though they may be, are people, too. As Plato said, "Be kind to everyone; dating is universally very bad!!"

But if something feels real to you, I think go ahead and make as much art as you can about it. Ultimately, women are punished whether or not they write about their relationships, and then to make it worse F. Scott Fitzgerald swoops in and steals their best lines. There's no good choice. I'm driven to write, so I'm going to write about my relationships. I mean, I'm certainly not going to write about the Napoleonic Wars. Napoleon was not hot!

Subtweets

Subtweets are tweets that are about specific people but don't explicitly name or tag those people.

I know that's a very *"Webster's Dictionary* defines 'subtweet' as . . ."* way to start a section, but guess what: *Webster's Dictionary* doesn't define subtweet as *anything*, because *Webster's Dictionary* apparently thinks it's too good for Twitter. (Though there's an argument that we're *all* too good for Twitter.) A dictionary that *doesn't* think it's too good for Twitter, or for honestly anything, is the *Oxford Dictionary*, they of "The word of the year for 2017 is 'youthquake'" fame. They are the dictionary equivalent of me learning the word "zaddy" from my teen brother in late 2016 and thinking I was on the cutting edge of culture. The *Oxford Dictionary* says what I said above but adds that subtweets are written "typically as a form of furtive mockery or criticism."

I really and truly think of most art as subtweets—it's about people, it usually doesn't explicitly name who it's about, very rarely do those people get notifications to alert them that art has been made about them, BUT generally when they encounter the art they have a pretty good idea what's up. But the second part of the *Oxford Dictionary*'s definition, the part about mockery and criticism, I'm not too sure about.

There is certainly a model of making art about your relationships where the aim is to punish men who have treated you badly. You're Carly Simon and Warren Beatty gets on your nerves and you write "You're So Vain" about him. And about two other people, whose identities we still don't know! If you leave things vague enough, you can manage to punish a handful of guys, just by implication. It doesn't really matter if it's about Mick Jagger or not: my mom has spent the last forty-four years telling everyone that it *is*, so at this point there's nothing Mick can do about it.

It is sometimes cathartic to use your art to PROVE that you have been wronged. There are definitely many ways in which we wrong one another in love, and seeing as men have vast structural power over women, I'd say that on balance men wrong women more. And beyond catharsis, excoriating an ex-lover can make one feel very of badass in a walking-away-from-an-explosion-in-a-tight-dress type of way. The eponymous Dick from *I Love Dick* once told

New York magazine that "the book was like a bad review of my presence in the world." I'll admit that, when I read that, I considered it what the kids used to refer to as "goals." Proving an injury through your art can feel especially rewarding when you have been trying to communicate something to a person and it's not working—they aren't listening to you, or they are but you can't get the ideas to make sense out loud in the way that they do in your brain. Or you're too afraid to tell someone in person! (I sometimes like to think of my subtweets existing in the vein of Frank O'Hara's Personism—a school of poetry that I THINK was meant to be a joke? But which is the best explanation I have ever heard for writing? It is poetry addressed to one person. O'Hara says he "founded" Personism when writing a poem for someone he was in love with, and "while I was writing it I was realizing that if I wanted to I could use the telephone instead of writing the poem.") You can take all the time in the world to communicate an idea through your art, or to use your art for proof of concept for something you feel but can't express. And then on top of that you get a song, or a novel, or— what other art is there? A woven blanket? And if your love interest sees that art and gets the hint, even better.

I no longer believe that the main purpose of art (or subtweets) is to punish men. Which is not to say I haven't at times used my tweets to do just that. But tweeting about a guy I don't talk to anymore does not make me feel GOOD and I don't WANT to do it, or at least not most of the time. It's coming from a reactionary place and it doesn't feel nourishing to me, though it is sometimes necessary to expel emotions from my body through tweeting, whereas others might expel those emotions through exercise or through traveling to a very deep and wide canyon and spending a couple hours screaming. Tweeting to shame or punish feels very Madame Defarge, who I don't really remember that much about beyond knowing that she is complicated but probably mostly wrong-headed. I think one of the most important purposes of art is to build empathy, and that doesn't come from considering one person in the story the absolute villain. Men can be goblins, yes, but they don't set out to be goblins. Just like how I don't set out to be a goblin, but somehow am one between 15 and 80 percent of the time! As Russian novelist and Nobel Laureate Aleksandr Solzhenitsyn wrote in *The Gulag Archipelago*: the line dividing good and evil cuts through the soul of every softboy.

So I'm not trying to punish individual men. I'm trying to blow up the power structures that allow them to systematically treat women like shit. When I write about discrete things men did to me that felt bad and gross, I hope that usually I am writing about them because I believe they are part of a larger pattern in this bedbug-infested quilt we call patriarchy. It's nothing PERSONAL! The idea is that other women will recognize similar incidents from their lives, and we can figure it out from there. That's a type of writing I find nourishing. I firmly believe that the personal is political, and that your specific softboy is a microcosm of society's softboy. It's comforting in the other direction, as well: when a man is doing very awful shit to me like wildly flirting with me and then standing me up to go hook up with other women, texting me a faux-sheepish brag-apology the next day, I like to think that he's not doing it because I in particular am a worthless, disposable rag, but because he is part of a larger population conditioned by society to act in this very rude way. I know it's wrong to try to change men, and instead of trying to change any individual man I try to change the culture that teaches these men how it's okay to behave. Probably not going to do me any immediate good, but maybe some girl born in 2040 will grow up and not have to put up with so many thoughtlessly hurtful texts from a man that she deletes their text history and starts responding "new phone, who dis."

Regardless of my good intentions, men immediately feel very attacked whenever I write about them. Even just quoting men in Instagram captions has provoked mini-breakdowns. And this, regardless of the actual content of the art! Maybe it's because they are so accustomed to controlling the narrative that losing that control for even a moment mega-freaks them out? Or maybe men assume that I must be out to punish or shame them—that my art serves a primarily negative purpose.

I think that men are reflexively suspicious of and uncomfortable with women writing about them because women are an oppressed group talking about their oppressors. Men have guilty consciences. And there's power and danger in women speaking honestly. Muriel Rukeyser wrote, "What would happen if one woman told the truth about her life? The world would split open." In 2017, we saw that that was true—except it had to be at least, like, ten women, and they had to be white and wealthy and famous. At the time I'm writing this, the world is still splitting open. It's shocking and heartening and necessary. I can see why men are scared of women writing truthfully about them. They should be.

As I said in the introduction of this book, which you didn't read because you assume all introductions are filler: I like men, especially the ones I smooch! But also, I feel a lot of emotions about *everything* (I will cry at any commercial—car, political campaign, whatever—that includes the Simon & Garfunkel song "America"), and when I meet a guy so hot that I feel the burning need to go see movies with him for the next forty years, you better believe I feel a ton of emotions about it. "I have instant conductors all over me," as Whitman said, which I will quote at every possible moment because I thought it was "I'm covered in electrodes" and I just recently rediscovered the actual wording. I need to put all those emotions to paper to understand them, to remember them, and because, as a friend once told me, I have "a compulsion to share details of my life." And I have to admit it hurts my delicate little feelings when men shiver like they've just heard two balloons rubbing together whenever they learn that I've written about them! This is who I am, I can't help it! I'd rather be a park ranger, but if I live in the middle of nature how am I ever going to get people to come to my comedy shows? So when men act all weirded out, it feels like they are rejecting a very large part of me. My whole personality is like: an artist, loves getting coffee with friends, and owns a skateboard but doesn't know how to use it. And also, these men *know* me. We've spent forty-five-minute subway rides back to their place where we've had to talk the *entire time*. Hopefully, at some point, they realize that I'm never going to excoriate them out of the blue. I'll at least send an email first!

Subtweets, Arranged by Who They Are About

MY HIGH SCHOOL CRUSH

[gives cute boy a mix CD with title "you are my boyfriend now"]
(June 19 2015)

i just googled my high school crush and a wedding website came up and honestly it was the platonic ideal of internet stalking
(Dec 31 2016)

i guess if i could go back and give my teenage self advice it would be to never laugh at anything a teenage boy said
(March 4 2017)

THE FIRST GUY I SLEPT WITH

my writing projects are like boyfriends, if i spend more than 3 hours with them in a row i decide i hate them
(May 30 2014)

A GUY I HAD A ROMANTIC FRIENDSHIP WITH FOR, LIKE, A YEAR AND NEVER KISSED

[tells kids story of how i fell in love w their dad] well we met in 2015 & for the next 3 years i wasn't sure if we were going on 'dates'
(June 9 2015)

trying to figure out how to kiss a boy without him knowing i want to kiss him
(July 1 2015)

my new favorite diss is to call guys a "classic Virgo" regardless of their actual birthday
(July 11 2015)

DUDE I KISSED TWICE AND WAS IN LOVE WITH FOR A YEAR

has anyone ever said "the plot thickens" about an actual crime and not about whether someone has a girlfriend
(Oct 6 2015)

Zayn said 1D music is 2 lame 2 to play on a date so clearly he doesnt realize forcing ur date 2 listen 2 shitty music u like is a power move
(Nov 15 2015)

if i could have dinner with 5 people living or dead i would def make the 4 greatest thinkers in history try to convince my crush to date me
(Jan 26 2016)

everyone is on their own path toward realizing they are in love with me
(Aug 23 2016)

GUY I SPENT MOST OF MY TIME WITH FOR A YEAR, THEN KISSED AND REALIZED I WAS BASICALLY IN LOVE WITH HIM, THEN CUT OUT OF MY LIFE

not only would i be in Ravenclaw but i would write a personal essay for the Daily Prophet about my unhealthy attraction to Slytherin boys
(Jan 29 2016)

writing fan fic about Watson telling Holmes
that their pseudoromantic friendship is making
him feel manipulated & they need 2 set
boundaries
(Feb 14 2016)

making a whole Lemonade about how i hate
Geminis
(May 11 2016)

No New Sociopaths
(May 26 2016)

the most interesting thing about MOST guys i
know is all the cool women they've dated
(July 1 2016)

all the women in New York are making dating
content about the same 5 men who work in
media
(Dec 5 2016)

hmmmmm should i spend this plane ride
reading a book or agonizing over why things
didn't work out w a person i stopped talking to
last year
(April 16 2017)

GUY I HOOKED UP WITH RIGHT AFTER TRUMP WAS ELECTED

tfw he criticizes Trump on social media before texting u back
(Nov 14 2016)

naming my book Who Cares If He's Just Not That Into You Or Not, Trump Is President, Jesus Christ
(Nov 15 2016)

is a first date too early to talk about how non violence only works if your oppressor has a conscience lol
(Nov 15 2016)

GUY WHO WENT ON MANY DATE-LIKE ACTIVITIES WITH ME BUT DENIES FLIRTING WITH ME

someone recently thanked me for publicly denying that we are dating so yes i am on top of the world
(June 26 2016)

i call men who don't want to date me "working class republicans" bc they are acting against their own interests
(July 12 2016)

If you don't like the new Harry Styles album you
are a misogynist (tweet 1/8,000,000)
(May 17 2017)

People Making Art About You

The flip side of making art about your relationships is that you have
to respect other people's right to make art about you.

There was a phase where I much rather would have been the
muse than the artist. In college, I asked my friend Todd if he would
rather be Neil Diamond and have written "Sweet Caroline," or be
Caroline Kennedy and have the song "Sweet Caroline" be about
you (at the time, "Sweet Caroline" was in my mind the epitome of
muse-inspired art in any medium). Todd, a good and hardwork-
ing boy, said Neil, but I emphatically wanted to be Caroline. She
has this great song about her, I thought, and she didn't have to do
any of the work! She did nothing and now Red Sox fans sing her
name every game. To be a muse is also proof, I thought, that someone loved you enough to create something deathless in your
honor. You've influenced them in a way they are not ashamed to
show to everyone. You're in art, which seemed exciting to me then
in a way it is still exciting to my parents whenever I'm on television for one nanosecond.

Now that I am a writer, I realize that I would have absolutely
no control over an artist's perception and interpretation of me and
whatever is between us. Which is likely annoying no matter what,

but especially so when you, too, are a person interested in telling stories and making art and immediately see how it could have been done RIGHT. As Caitlin Moran told Terry Gross, she realized as a young woman that "if anyone was going to write a song or, you know, or a book, or make a film about a girl like me, it was going to have to be a girl like me, and quite literally, me."

When I read or watch anything comedic, my mind immediately goes to how I would have done it differently and better (usually the answer is a bigger mustache). For art about my relationships, not only do I have an opinion on the jokes, I also have an opinion on how I acted, how he acted, what my "vibe" is, how exactly everything went down, what it all means, and what's the best way to present it. I'm going to want to make art about it, and I'm going to make the best art I possibly can, so there's a very good chance that the art he makes is, in my opinion, not the correct or best version! (Unless he's a better artist than me, in which case I may believe it is a better version than mine, but still not correct.)

I also realize nothing is ever really about the muse, that if a guy were to "make art about me" I would really just be his jumping-off point. Assuming otherwise is what freaks men out about women's art, I think—they're like, "Holy shit, she wrote about me, she must be deeply in love with me." After all, you did spend so much time on it, time you could have spent eating ice cream and watching *Paddingtons 1 & 2*. But in my experience, art "about a specific person" is really a consideration of either myself or society (or both) that stems from one thing a dude did; I would guess that in many cases when women make art about men they care more about the art than they do about the men. Like, there is no way Beyoncé loves Jay-Z more than her art. I'm sure she loves Blue Ivy, Rumi, and Sir more than her art, but not Jay-Z.

ALSO, not to be a capitalist hack, but the problem with being Caroline Kennedy is NEIL DIAMOND GETS ALL THE MONEY.

I no longer think that making art about a person is the biggest sign that you love them; right now I think love is carving out big chunks of time to focus solely on that person. But sometimes, reading about my female artistic idols, I envy the creative-romantic partnerships they had. Patti Smith, a woman with impeccable taste in men, writes in *Just Kids* that she imagined herself "as Frida to Diego, both muse and maker."

So I do support anyone's right to make art about me. And I think I'd genuinely love if a man whose art I admired and whose bod I also admired found in me inspiration for his songs or cartoons or hell, even tweets. I'm sure it would also feel very weird, like a foot falling asleep, or that part of getting a pap smear when you feel like you're getting electrocuted on a part of your body you had never even felt before. This is all theoretical for now, because no man has made art about me, THAT WE KNOW OF, YET. On balance, I do hope it happens. And I hope it's Harry Styles's sophomore album.

The Pay Is Certain

Here's what solace I have in being single and being ambiguously coupled and being coupled but suspecting you're to some extent incapable of emotional connection (ask me about the painting my mom commissioned of my siblings and me when we were young, when she had the artist paint me standing far away because "oh, you're emotionally distant"): no matter what happens, you can always write your way through. As Walt Whitman said, in a poem about unrequited love:

> *But now I think there is no unreturn'd love, the pay is*
> *   certain one way or another*
> *(I loved a certain person ardently, and my love was*
> *   not return'd,*
> *Yet out of that I have written these songs.)*

Even if things truly suck ass (and no disrespect to sucking ass!), you will always have your art. And please note: I don't mean this in a career way where it's like "that ding-dong treated me like shit and I wrote a wildly popular HBO sitcom about it!" (a) I don't view writing as a weapon, and I generally feel like most stories don't have one "villain" with the exception of any story about any member of the Trump family. (b) It is extremely annoying to me that when bad things happen to nonwriters, everyone else is like, "Oh my god, I'm so sorry, are you okay?" but when bad things happen to me, a writer, everyone is like, "Ha ha ha, you can write about this!" It always feels like the subtext is "You can use this as material to get rich and famous!" but I'd like to think I can think up material without having to suffer. And if never suffering meant that I'd never get to be a writer, like how Matilda loses her powers after she's not being neglected and abused anymore, HONESTLY I'D BE TOTALLY HAPPY BEING A LAWYER.

What "You'll always have your art" or "You can always write your way through this" or "The pay is certain" means for me is that you can create something genuinely good out of your experiences, however shitty. I mean it in that hippy-dippy way that sounds totally fake and dumb to me until I sit down and think about it: that art is really about figuring out how to order and process the events of your life. For me, that means finding a way in which things are funny, because otherwise I let myself wallow in self-pity and I become depressed and ashamed of my failure and I start to fixate on, like, whether I've been too much of a financial drain on my parents, who *barely* asked for this. For other people, it might be just ordering the chaos into a story that makes people (or yourself!) cry and/or laugh, so that someone at some point is getting some enjoyment out of it. And that—telling stories to your screaming friends—is something EVERYONE does, not just artists.

Like: I recently moved into a semi-poison apartment where the landlord does the exact opposite of any maintenance job, like the "Monkey's Paw" version of a plumber. (I asked him to make the shower pipe stop shooting water at the ceiling and now it shoots water absolutely everywhere EXCEPT the ceiling??) I was feeling alone and ashamed and getting constant stress cold sores— and then my aunt, laughing, read me a paragraph from a Sloane Crosley essay about a deranged (rude) teen neighbor, in which Sloane points out that New Yorkers consider murder before they consider moving. And I realized: wow, this woman, who is so much more successful and elegantly named than I, has similar problems. And one day, women who spend a year and a half pretending they aren't in love with someone and then realize they are and then freak out and blow their whole life up might feel slightly less horrible knowing that the same thing happened to a beautiful writer named Blythe, right before her rotten ceiling fell in and killed her after the landlord refused to fix it.

And so hopefully you and your romantic partner will treat each other lovingly and tenderly and hopefully you will come up with weird extended bits that alienate everyone, and probably you will both be total cunts to each other at certain points, and probably if you're a woman attracted to dudes they'll fuck you over with their privilege, whether they realize they're doing that or not. Whatever happens will happen, but the pay is certain: you'll always be able to write, or talk, or paint, or knit (why do people knit??) about it. You can make it into something beautiful or hilarious or genius or so incredibly dumb that it's hilarious and genius.

You'll get better each time, as a writer/painter/whatever and as a person. And regardless of whether I am forever alone until I fall into the Grand Canyon and die (likely) or end up in a very happy relationship (less likely), I will always have that. In fact, that's why I got a tattoo that says "the pay is certain." Everyone thinks my tattoo is a mob thing. Still trying to write my way through that one.

CONCLUSION

Well, friends. I thought so long and so hard about romance and dating that I am now living with my very hot boyfriend in the middle of nowhere (New Mexico). I will never be unhappy for another moment in my life. I spend my days walking around saving baby squirrels who have fallen out of their nests while my boyfriend builds mountains of furniture out of reclaimed wooden milk crates. Honestly, things have worked out pretty great on my end! Thanks for reading.

I mean, okay, yeah, obviously not. Though it does seem like every book about the impossibility of dating ends with the author revealing she met a man and, during the course of her writing, married him, I've somehow made it out of this whole thing without a husband or even a boyfriend! But I'm pretty stoked to keep trying to get men to kiss me while not oppressing me. Failing that, simply not oppressing me is a good starting point! I thought I'd come out of this book happy and excited to never have to think about dating again, to move on and spend the rest of my life learning bizarre animal facts. (Ask me how many distinct species of moth have been found living on just one sloth.) (Seven!) In actuality, I'm more convinced than ever that love and romance and, ugh, "dating" are important and smart things to think and write about.

If 60 percent of my romantic neuroses come from watching rom-coms and wanting my life to conform to narrative structures, then maybe it's on me to change those structures through my writing? I mean, ordering things into a narrative is necessary to have a coherent sense of self and to move through the world. That's a real thing, I learned it in AP Psychology. If you'd like it in a vaguer (but good) quote from David Foster Wallace: "We need narrative like we need space-time: it's a built-in thing." Coming up with narrative structures that are not only entertaining but also socially responsible is one of the actually long-term useful things that writers can do. Obviously much of the writing I do is just frivolous reactions to whatever Timo Chalamet did that day, but I'd like to think I can imagine narratives that change the way we think about how love might look.

We've got one go on this floating orange to squeeze out as much happiness as we can, and love is a pretty significant citrus press. A journalist once asked Nora Ephron why she wrote only about relationships, and she responded, "Is there something else?" You know, there's hanging out with your homies. There's doing work that is meaningful to you. There's helping other people. There's looking at very steep mountains and being, like, [crying] "It is so steep and . . . beautiful." And there's love. There really isn't anything else.

Acknowledgments

This is my first book, so basically: thank you to everyone I have ever met.

I am incredibly indebted to my brilliant agent, Dana Murphy. Thank you for wanting to work with me before I even had an idea for a book, when I just waltzed into a Maison Kayser wearing my own wedding dress and left screaming, "I'm late for drinks with [hot guy]—he's the entire book!!" (He's mentioned, like, twice?) Thank you for encouraging the idea kernel I gave to you and patiently helping me refine it over the literal YEAR it took me to write my proposal. I was a dumb baby who had truly zero idea what she was doing, and none of this would have even been close to happening if not for you.

Kara Rota: Without you, this book would not exist. Or it would, but it wouldn't be finished until 2067, would be very stupid, and would consist entirely of the word "literally" and references to Timothée Chalamet. I feel like a smarter and better person from having worked with you. Thanks for letting me text you at midnight about the book and also about whether I had strep or a throat STI. (It was "light mono.") I AM GLAD WE ARE FRIENDS.

Thank you also to Bryn Clark for not only editorial help but also the genius title of this book, which is everyone's favorite thing about it. Any success it has is owed to you.

Also at Flatiron, and beyond: Nancy Trypuc, Patricia Cave, Na Kim, Bethany Reis (sorry for stet-ing so many double exclamation marks!!!!), Emily Walters, and Lena Shekhter.

A massive thank-you to Phoebe Robinson. Your check-ins and encouragement kept me going when this book felt fake or unruly or like it was just never, ever going to be finished. Thank you for demystifying for me the whole weirdo process of writing a book, and for showing me that it was even possible in the first place. You have been so generous with your ever-dwindling free time, and it means a lot to me.

Thank you to Emma Allen. There is a straight line between you publishing me and anything else good that has ever happened in my professional life. And honestly, many of the good things that have happened in my personal life. I feel very lucky that you exist!

To all my coworkers at *The Late Show*, for making every day at work fun and for dealing with me as I ran around with galleys of my book, screaming. Cami, my beauty angel!! Dom, who has taught me to use Instagram! Gloria, thank you for hiring me and finding me a place to live! Monica and my manager, Neil, for letting me come sit in your office for great stretches of time for no reason. Caroline for never being too busy to talk about whether, for example, Giovanni Ribisi is hot (no). Ali and Carly and Kyle and Megan and Cohen and everyone who has ever been a PA. Stephen, for blurbing this book, and Amy for making that happen. EVERY-ONE ON STAFF. Pizza!

A big thank-you to all of my friends who listened to me talking about this book for five hundred thousand years, and to all the friends I bailed on because I had a deadline, like, two days ago. To Lily Karlin and Madelyn Freed and Colin Stokes and everyone on Lo-Fi for writing and performing with me, and to Todd Venook, Emmy Yates, Molly Yates, and Rebecca Margolies just because. Special thanks to those friends who let me quote their genius ideas: Zach Zimmerman (feel free to give him money at Venmo: @zach-zimmerman), Paul Gale (like and subscribe to youtube.com/paulgalecomedy), Harris Mayersohn (whose quality Twitter @harrismayer you should NEVER mute or he will threaten to stop being your friend), and Fran Hoepfner (franhoepfner.fyi). Also Jonah who is bad at the internet and probably doesn't want me to list his last name.

There was a point at which I was keeping a list of all the women who have helped me along the way, but I lost the list. So I know I'm forgetting many, but thank you to Jocelyn Richard, Jen Spyra, Marla Tepper, Kim Gamble, Nikki Glaser, Sara Schaefer, Jenny Hagel, Ariel Dumas, and Jennifer Mills.

Obviously the biggest thanks go to my family for raising me and loving me and always, always encouraging me to pursue my dreams. I am one of those rare, lucky people whose family never made a crack about English degrees not being useful or writing being impossible to break into. Thank you for unconditionally supporting me as I wrote this book, even though I told you all not to read it. Thanks for letting me hang out at your house and eat your food as I "wrote" (watched full seasons of prestige dramas). I love you all so, so, so much. I won the family lottery. Please stop texting me so much on the group text thread.